Shadows of Heroes

Shadows of Heroes

The Journey of a Doctor and a Journalist in the Lives of Ordinary People Who Became Victims of Torture

Miron Varouhakis, Ph.D.

To order additional copies of this book, contact:
Xlibris Corporation
1-888-795-4274
www.Xlibris.com
Orders@Xlibris.com
78593

Contents

This book is dedicated to all of those who lost their life in faraway places while providing humanitarian assistance to fellow humans who were experiencing the cruelty of war. Humanity is poorer without them . . . .

ACKNOWLEDGEMENTS

I would like to give my utmost gratitude to Dr. Maria Piniou-Kalli, whose steady support and guidance made this book a reality. She has been a constant inspiration to me and her work has strengthened my resolve to keep working towards a torture-free world.

A special thanks also goes to Robert White, the former representative of the U.N. High Commissioner for Refugees in Greece, who wrote an analysis on asylum and immigration for the book. His expertise and opinions provided a vigorous examination of a very complex issue that cuts across borders and cultures, while his first-hand knowledge of the region offered a colorful portrayal of the situation.

Of course I cannot emphasize enough how grateful I am to all the torture survivors and refugees who allowed me into their lives and shared with me the darkest tales of their life. This book was written for them in hope that their voices will help break the silence that has traditionally surrounded torture. They are the true heroes and it is time for all of us to acknowledge their existence and protect them.

Finally, I would like to thank all those who one way or another helped make this book possible, including the staff of the Medical Rehabilitation Council for Torture Victims (MRCT) in Athens, the staff of the UNHCR in Greece and the International Rehabilitation Council for Torture Victims (IRCT) in Copenhagen.

INTRODUCTION

This book is not a novel. It is perhaps one of the most challenging approaches that have been made in recent years on the sensitive subject of torture, as it is centered on the personal testimonies of actual torture victims as they were recorded by an anti-torture doctor and a journalist—who also is the author of this book.

The book is an attempt to present both the current and timeless dimensions of torture across the world by recording testimonies of victims from the Middle East, Asia, North Africa, Europe, as well as North and South America.

Torture is a subject that touches upon the darkest sides of the human soul—that of the torturer that the system itself has created—since it reveals in the most grotesque way the incredible barbarity that is hidden inside humans.

An Irish priest who was captured and tortured in Argentina in the late 1970s notes that "torture has no limits to what they can do to you," both physically and psychologically.

The issues of impunity, the transfer of torture methods, the legal framework and the international treaties, asylum, the war against terrorism and the violation of human rights are only some of the issues that this book is attempting to present through testimonies and the recording of current affairs.

From Afghanistan to Guantanamo Bay, and from Iraq to the United States, the book is following step by step the events through testimonies, official records and news reports, revealing that way the complete and true picture of human rights worldwide.

The title of the book, "Shadows of Heroes," was chosen because these two simple words capture perhaps the two largest truths of torture victims: heroism and anonymity. The victims are survivors. They are ordinary people who have exhibited unparallel heroism by having survived the most hideous torture acts that most of us can't even fathom. At the same time, though, for the rest of us they are shadows of people, who remain nameless and faceless, as they have found shelter in their anonymity.

Those who do survive soon discover that the journey to freedom can be equally brutal. As if they had not suffered enough at the hands of their torturers, these 'human shadows' sell all their belongings and embark on a deadly journey of illegal immigration as cargo in the back of a truck or on a boat, a path that is governed by ruthlessness and a multi-billion human trafficking industry. Those who are lucky enough not to drown in choppy seas or killed in minefield-infested borders are then faced with another calamity, that of asylum. The vast majority of them will discover the cruel reality that in the industrialized world 'humanity' is a commodity, and asylum-seekers are stocks that are traded on a global market of migration. The bulk of asylum-seekers see their applications rejected by a growing number of countries, and soon find themselves deported back to their countries, to their torturers.

Although the subject of torture is an issue that we humans have been pondering over since the time of Aristotle in ancient Greece, today only a minority of people are aware of the graveness of the problem worldwide. This is the reason for writing this book.

The idea for the book was born some 10 years ago when I was still working as a newspaper reporter for *Kathimerini English Edition*—a daily newspaper published by Greece's leading morning daily in a joint partnership with the *International Herald Tribune*. One day I went to cover a news conference at the Medical Rehabilitation Center for Torture Victims in Athens, the existence of which until that day I was ignoring—just like most people at the time.

As soon as I walked into the anti-torture center I was grabbed by a sense of tension and tranquility that was emanating from the place. It was as if you knew that a few hours ago some very special people had walked through that same room, but you couldn't exactly understand why their presence was still noticeable.

But perhaps what captured my attention the most was the personality of the medical-director of the rehabilitation center, Dr. Maria Piniou-Kalli—the doctor in this book. It was exactly the opposite of what I expected. With a fresh smile on her face and the strength of soul and energy of a young kid, she welcomed the reporters as if she was having a group of friends at her house. This immediacy and sincerity of her character won me from the first moment. Free from the customary pomposity, Maria with her simplicity of character managed in a few minutes to revive the human values that have been rapidly fading from the human culture. It soon became obvious to me that she had lived through some very unique experiences and had a very strong spirit, from which she was drawing all that energy for her and for everyone else in the room.

Soon, our cooperation was broaden due to an increase of human rights violations in several countries around the world, and not long after I found myself offering my services as a volunteer to the center and writing a number of press releases. This allowed me to come even closer to the torture victims by participating in the weekly sessions of the anti-torture center where all the recent cases were reviewed and evaluated in order to decide which cases were genuine and would merit a "certificate of torture victim." Those certificates are of immense value, not only because they are recognized by the government, but also because the certified torture victims are almost guaranteed asylum in the country.

Every time Maria would come back to Greece from her visits to various countries as president of the International Rehabilitation Council of Torture Victims—a Copenhagen-based umbrella group with over 200 anti-torture centers around the world—we would get together and record her experiences, some of which are included in this book.

My life had changed! Hope this book helps change yours as well . . .

Miron Varouhakis, Ph.D.
Columbia, January 2010

JOURNEY TO DEATH

The young social worker opened the iron gate that was leading into the front yard of the building and escorted the reporter and the interpreter to the front door of the house. As they walked through the front yard the reporter observed the frail condition of the building—a sign of abandonment. The small garden was covered with parched plants that were hugging the ground, resembling an old man waiting for death and salvation. The exterior walls stood as witnesses of how harsh time has been with them: Chinks—like deep knife wounds on a human flesh—had stripped away most of the color and façade, revealing the naked bricks that had turn green from the dampness. A sprayed red sign on the wall by the civil protection agency warned that the building was unfit for habitation.

The door of the house opened and the reporter was faced with a large number of men, women, and children who were sitting on the floor on top of blankets and unfolded pieces of cardboard boxes. Those were and the only objects in the room, which was surrounded by crumbling walls. The reporter paused for a moment, noticing how the eyes of the people were glowing with fortitude in spite the fact that signs of destitute and hunger were evident on their bodies and clothing as they were resting on the ground. After they greeted everyone and took off their shoes, the visitors entered the second room, which was also empty aside from a blanket and some pieces of cardboard boxes on the floor—used as an insulator for the dampness during these cold days of December. The reporter took a quick glance inside and saw three men sitting on the floor in the middle of the room drinking hot tea—one of them was Ayiad. A tall, swarthy, middle-aged man with a moustache, Ayiad stood out from the other two men as the leading figure in the room. Born in Iraq—like the rest of the people who had found shelter in the abandoned building in central Athens—Ayiad had come recently to Greece with his family in order to escape persecution from the regime of Saddam Hussein. They were among thousands of Iraqis who had come illegally in the country to seek asylum.

The reporter, who knew beforehand that he would be interviewing a torture survivor, greeted Ayiad with a handshake and sat next to him, forming a circle with the other two men, the interpreter and the social worker. Wearing clothes from donations to humanitarian organizations that were meant for a person twice his weight and half his height, Ayiad welcomed the reporter with a bright smile as if it was a social visit by an old friend on a Sunday evening. "Bring some tea to offer our guests," Ayiad said to the women in the next room as if he was receiving guests at his house in Baghdad. Nothing was hinting at the unspeakable horror that this man had endure.

Surprised by the strength of his spirit, the reporter told the interpreter to ask Ayiad if he would agree to use a tape recorder for the interview. It was the first time Ayiad would speak publicly about his torture by Saddam Hussein's security forces, and the reporter wanted to be careful in his every move. Besides, the year was 2002 and Saddam Hussein was still in power. "Of course," replied Ayiad while gesturing with his hands to the reporter to place the tape recorder on the ground in front of him. As he was placing the recording device, the reporter noticed that a sense of pride had been sketched in Ayiad's face as the interview was about to start. "I was not always in this condition as you see me here today," Ayiad told the reporter with a serene and gentle look in his eyes as the guest was accepting a cup of hot tea from the hands of an Iraqi woman. "I was a professor at the University of Baghdad and I was living with my family in a nice, big house not far out from the city."

Born in 1951 in the city of Kirkuk—about 220 kilometers (136 miles) north of Baghdad—Ayiad, although a Turkoman and a Sunni Muslim, managed to climb the social-class ladder of the Iraqi society, reaching levels that were occupied mainly by the dominant Shiites. An academic position at the art school meant recognition, respect and a middle-class status that he never thought attainable while growing up in Kirkuk. Because of his position at the university, he frequently attended dinners and cocktail receptions at the mansions of prominent Iraqis. It was like a daydream. But, like any dream it did not last long, and in Ayiad's case it soon turned into a nightmare.

One day in 1989 and while Ayiad was at the university, a group of students who were representing a student organization—which as he notes its members included undercover agents of state security services—approached him and asked him to build a glorious statue of Iraqi President Saddam Hussein. For Ayiad, 38 at the time, the project appeared overwhelming—both in scale and significance. Fearing that his craftsmanship could prove meager in reflecting his leader's glory, as well as of the penalties that could follow such failure, he declined. Besides, he was well aware that artists who had fail to reflect the Saddam's leadership in their work had soon after met their death.

Little did he know that his decision instead of protecting him would earn him a ticket to the darkest journey of his life, filled with humiliation, torture and near-death experiences. He would soon share the fate of thousands of Iraqi torture victims.

A few days after the visit to his office by members of the student group, Ayiad received another visit, this time by secret police agents. Ayiad was arrested and taken to a detention center in downtown Baghdad where he would spend the next nine months and thirteen days in isolation.

"They placed me inside a red-painted room no larger than 1 meter by 3 meters (3 feet by 10 feet) which had a toilet in the middle and no windows," said Ayiad as he was trying to tighten his belt and pull together his clothes that had started to get loose. "They had me locked in there for as many as 19 days without anyone coming and explaining to me why I had been arrested," he added as he paused to drink some tea.

One day his interrogation started and along with it his torture . . .

"They blindfolded me and took me to the basement. The first question they asked me was: 'where are the bombs you were going to use?' Puzzled as I was because I was blindfolded, I asked them: 'Are you talking to me?'" he said. He tried in vain to explain that he had nothing to do with any bombs and any plot for a popular revolt. That is when the nightmare begun. His answers enraged his interrogators who soon became his torturers. In the days, weeks and months that followed, his interrogators used batons to beat him, administered electroshocks to his genitalia and ears, drilled on his heels, sunken him in tank filled with sewer wastes, and placed him in a coffin to be buried alive. Ayiad explained that each interrogation session would last up to four hours.

"When they administer electroshocks in the ears you lose control of your jaws," said Ayiad while gesturing to the women to leave the room in order to show the scars on his body. "When they performed electroshocks in my genitalia I felt the bones in my spine to crack."

With the women having left the room, Ayiad stood up and slowly removed both of his socks, revealing a gruesome spectacle to the reporter who was sitting next to him: both heels exhibited deep round wounds that reached the bone. "They used a drilling machine and pushed it hard so it would go deeper and deeper into the bone. Every time they did that I would pass out from the pain," said Ayiad as the memories from the painful experience started to overtake the expressions on his face.

Without wasting any time, Ayiad started to remove his shirt to expose the numerous wounds that were still clearly visible even after a decade. Scars and deformities were present across his upper body. As he explained through the translator, his torturers tied his hands behind his back and pulled him up high with a rope until his shoulders and wrists were dislocated and he screamed in pain. "In spite all of this, I didn't say anything. There was nothing to say," said Ayiad, who until today cannot fathom why he had to go through this horrendous nightmare.

As the days were passing his interrogation and torture were becoming part of his daily routine until one day he could no longer feel his body from the pain. It was then that they called for an ambulance. But as Ayiad realized soon after, the ambulance was not heading to the nearest hospital but a cemetery. "They asked me at which cemetery I would like to be buried and I told them that I would like to be buried in my hometown. But they ignored my request and instead said they would take me to a cemetery in Gazalia—an area in western Baghdad where word in the street had it that it was the burial ground for many victims of torture," said Ayiad while trying to put his shirt back on.

After a while the ambulance arrived at the cemetery and they immediately started to remove his clothes. A few minutes later they placed him naked inside a coffin to be buried alive. "I could hear the nails being hammered on the cover of the coffin while at the same time I had the feeling that I was hearing the voice of my seven-year-old daughter yelling: 'Bear up! Bear up! Bear up!'" Ayiad said. "I was waiting to die. I could no longer feel my body." As Ayiad explained to the reporter, after a few hours a man came and opened the coffin and was surprised to see that he was still alive. "A tall, thin, and swarthy man opened the coffin and asked me: 'You haven't died yet?'"

Ayiad was then taken out of the coffin, was given back his clothes, and he was driven back to the detention center and to his room with the number 21. The period of his interrogation would last two more months and then he would be transferred to a larger cell where he would join some 70 more detainees. His transfer to the new cell will also mark the beginning of his trial before one of the notorious revolutionary courts of Baghdad. His first day in court would come little over nine months after his arrest.

But Ayiad's physical condition had become so frail that he had to be transported in an ambulance and wheeled into the courtroom. Ayiad recalled that one of the officers who escorted him into the courtroom that day was a former student at the university where he had been teaching, a fact that confirmed his suspicions that members of the student organization had been behind his arrest. The former "student" even advised Ayiad to plea guilty to all the charges.

Soon after the hearing started Ayiad realized that he could no longer stand the parody that surrounded the entire process. As the prosecutor was addressing the court and presented the charges against him, Ayiad started to take off his clothes. "As he was making his speech I started to undress. The judge saw me and asked me what I was doing, and I told him: 'My body is completely broken. Just look at my body . . . I have nothing else to say," said Ayiad while looking the reporter straight into his eyes.

As he explained in court later in his testimony the reason he declined to build the statue of Saddam Hussein was because he did not believe enough in his artistic abilities and was afraid of the consequences if he failed. "They thought that I didn't want to make the statue because I didn't want Saddam Hussein, but that was not the reason," Ayiad told the court. "All Iraqis say 'yes' to Saddam Hussein and you parasite said 'no?'" the judge remarked according to Ayiad. The judge then asked him: "'Dog, to how many years you would like me to sentence you?' I told him to sentence me to 10 years, but he said: 'No! I will give you 20 years so that you get reformed and become an example for all Turkomans.'"

Sitting in his wheelchair, Ayiad thanked the judge for sparing his life and not sentencing him to death. Soon after the judge had rendered his ruling, the security guards who had escorted Ayiad to the courthouse wheeled him again onto the ambulance and took him back to his cell at the detention center. He remained there for another two weeks before he was transferred to a prison, the name of which was not disclosed to him or his family. It was only after he managed to smuggle a letter out of the prison that his wife learned where he was being held.

Ayiad would spend one year in prison. He will be released on Aug. 17, 1991, after Saddam Hussein gave amnesty to a number of political prisoners as a goodwill gesture after his forces captured Kuwait _ as he did again on Oct. 20, 2002, as a way of thanking the nation for re-electing him the week prior.

But Ayiad's homecoming was not trouble-free. After his release from prison Ayiad would visit his old department at the University of Baghdad only to find out that he could no longer have his old job back. It was then that he decided to return to his hometown and open a small workshop.

As he poured in some more hot tea for him and his visitors, Ayiad explained that the years after his release from prison were especially harsh for his family, both financially and socially, as they were carrying the stigma of being dissidents. Their friends were few and his clients even fewer. Ayiad explained that people were afraid to be seen with him or his family because they could be accused of having ties with dissidents and rebels.

Five years later, in 1996, the Iraqi people will be called to vote "Yes" or "No" for keeping Saddam Hussein in power in just another of the so-called presidential elections. Ayiad—outraged by the ill-treatment, torture, suffering, and unjust prosecution he faced from members of Hussein's security and judicial apparatus—decided to vote "No" even though he knew that the voting process was not that secret.

But, the price of his decision to cast a "No" vote—which in any civilized country would fall under a citizen's democratic right—will not come cheap. About a year later, on June 9, 1997, members of the state security services will arrest him again. Ayiad will be held for questioning at a local police station for five days before being transferred at a detention center in Baghdad—the same one where he had been held some eight years ago. "There, they interrogated me but they did not torture me again because I was already crippled," said Ayiad with a tone of pride that was stemming from the wounds of torture that had scarred his body.

After his second arrest his family sold all their belongings—including a car, jewelry, and Ayiad's paintings—in order to raise 18 million dinars that was needed to bribe a security guard for his release. Upon his "release"—which would come three months after his arrest—Ayiad would take his family and return to his hometown, where they will stay only briefly as they feared further persecution from Saddam's regime. Using $50,000 that a relative of his sent him from Switzerland, Ayiad would take his family and flee Iraq. The journey out of Iraq will not be risk-free. First, they had to travel through northern Iraq—which was under Kurdish control—without being detected by government security forces. From there, they had to travel to Turkey in the back of a truck and then cross into Greece illegally on foot.

But their arrival to Greece did not mark the end of their arduous journey as they had anticipated. Ayiad and his family will be arrested by Greek border guards for entering illegally into the country, and will be held for three months at a detention facility in northern Greece. On the day of their release Greek authorities ordered them to leave the country within 15 days or face a forced deportation.

By the time Ayiad met with the reporter, in December 2002, he and his family had been in Greece for little over four months, moving from city to city and from building to building to avoid police detection. But for the last month they managed to stay put in the same abandoned building in this poor neighborhood of Athens, with no water or electricity. Still, every day they lived with the fear and someone always had to be on the lookout as the police made routine inspections in the area for drugs and undocumented immigrants.

"Last night they came again and marched us out in the street and told us to leave from here," said Ayiad, noting that apparently some of the neighbors had called in and complained to the police about them. But Ayiad did not appear to be intimidated. Rather he seemed to be in high spirits. "As soon as we are granted asylum we will go to Switzerland and find my relatives there," he added with a tone of firmness.

The reporter, sitting cross-legged on a dirty blanket on the floor of this dilapidated building, watched Ayiad with admiration but also with wonderment. He could not fathom where this man found the strength in his spirit to reclaim his just right to life after that brutal torture and unspeakable abuse of his body and soul that almost led to his death. The answer—although simple—will come the next day.

"You are a hero! The fact that you are here today and you are alive is heroic," a doctor told Ayiad while she was reviewing his medical report and history during his visit at the Medical Rehabilitation Center for Torture Victims (MRCT)[1] in Athens.

It was a heroism that is unparallel to the kind of definition that has been generally ascribed to the word by most known dictionaries. He was not a member of an outnumbered infantry unit that fought with remarkable bravery as it charged and seized control of a strategic location. He was not a member of an armed resistance group that defeated a junta or an invader. He was not awarded a medal for bravery over his self-sacrifice in rescuing a fellow soldier amidst heavy firefight. It is the heroism of an ordinary person who went through a living hell for a simple "no" he said one day, which could have been just another Monday.

Ayiad _ whose real name has been withheld to protect his identity and that of his family _ has been recognized as a torture victim by the Medical Rehabilitation Center for Torture Victims (MRCT) in Athens.

---

[1] The medical rehab center is a member of the Copenhagen-based International Rehabilitation Council for Torture Victims (IRCT), an umbrella anti-torture organization with more than 200 centers worldwide. Operating in Greece since 1989 with funding from the European Union, the MRCT has been examining and treating hundreds of torture cases each year. The alleged victims are examined by a network of some 35 specialized doctors affiliated with the center, and if their story is verified medically then the center grants them a certificate identifying them as a victim of torture. The certificate, recognized by Greek authorities, ensures that the victim will be granted asylum in the country.

Iraq for years has been toping the list of countries of origin for torture victims visiting the rehab center, a clear manifestation of the ongoing atrocities carried out by Saddam's regime against his own people. In 2000 alone, 56 out of 139 cases that were treated at the anti-torture center involved Iraqis, accounting for over 40 percent of the center's patients. According to Amnesty International, prior to the removal of Saddam Hussein by the U.S.-led forces in 2003 the torture of political prisoners was systematic. In its 2001 report the human rights watchdog noted that some of the most common torture methods were the use of electroshock in various parts of the body; beatings with batons, metal pipes, whips and other devices; beating on the sole of the feet (phalanx); the uprooting of nails from the hands and feet; group rape and sexual abuse with the use of various objects; mock executions; and the drilling of feet and hands.

The regime of Saddam Hussein left behind thousands of torture victims—some of them dead and some alive—and along with them an open social wound to remind Iraqis and the rest of the world the barbarity that is hidden in the human soul.

Today, the torture rehab center cares for over 1,000 victims, both men and women, and nearly half of them are from Iraq.

"Unsystematic beatings, all forms of hangings, electroshocks and phalanx continue to be some of the most commonly used tortured methods in Iraq today," noted Dr. Maria Piniou-Kalli, former president of the IRCT and current medical director at the rehab center in Athens, after she met with Ayiad.

With a torture victim certificate from MRCT in hand _ guarantying asylum in Greece _ Ayiad and his family hope that their ordeal is now over. Without it he would have been just another digit in the rising number of asylum-seekers in the country whose application is still pending or has been denied.

Wearing the clothes he received from donations wrapped around his body like a drape and sitting in a deep couch at the office of Dr. Piniou-Kalli, Ayiad appeared to take courage from the comforting words of the doctor—not that he was in need of it, as he seemed to have more than enough for at least a dozen more people.

But his name will not be written in newspapers as the reporter, although extremely inspired by the interview and the material he gathered, he will decide to refrain from publishing it, and thus Ayiad would continue to live in the anonymity of his heroism. The reason behind the reporter's decision was that during the period he conducted the interview the governments of the United States and Great Britain were collecting reports on human rights violations by Saddam Hussein's regime and were using them as one of the justifications to attack Iraq. So, the reporter felt that the publishing of Ayiad's story instead of sensitizing people over the continuing use of torture in Iraq would rather become ammunition in the arsenal of the two governments seeking to legalize their military intervention.

Besides, Ayiad's anonymity had been guaranteed even if the story had been published as the name "Ayiad" was an alias that was chosen jointly by him and the reporter for his own protection and of his family. Hence, until today he remains a shadow of a hero.

THE DOCTOR

The encouraging words that Ayiad heard from the lips of the doctor at the Medical Rehabilitation Center for Torture Victims (MRCT) in Athens didn't sound as arbitrary and they did not appear to be hot air. In Ayiad's eyes—which were fixed on Maria—her compassion toward him was unlike anything he had encountered in his meetings with other doctors. He could not explain it, but in his mind knew that this kind of compassion could come only from a person who had been the target of an unjust and cruel persecution similar to his.

Indeed, Maria was not just an ordinary dermatologist who one day decided to devote a large part of her life in the treatment and protection of torture survivors. She was the kind of a woman who learned the true meaning of state persecution ever since she was a little girl, and who grew up to give her own meaning to the word "hero."

From the years of the Resistance[2], the political persecutions during the Civil War[3], the assassination of Greek leftist politician Grigoris Lambrakis[4], the junta [5]and the exile of thousands of Greek Communists, Maria was an eyewitness as she was directly involved due to the activities of her father and later of her own as members of leftists movements. Born on the tiny island of Thassos in northern Greece and in a poor family which espoused the Communist ideology—at a time when the country was in search for its own lost identity—Maria will come face-to-face with the Resistance

---

[2] The Resistance in Greece started in 1941 and ended in 1944. At the time Greece was occupied by German-Nazi forces—which were deployed in central and southern Greece—and Bulgarian forces in the north. The Greek resistance came to life in the form of three groups: the guerrillas of EAM-ELAS who were led by the Greek Communist Party and who were deployed mainly in northern Greece; the PAO (Pan-Greek Liberation Organization) resistance group in the southern German sector; and the guerrillas of Anton Tsaous in the north.

[3] The Greek Civil War was fought between 1942 and 1949 and it pitted some 100,000-strong force of Greek Army, Royalist forces and British troops from one side and some 20,000 Communist guerrillas on the other. The government forces had the support of the United States and Britain, while the Communist guerrillas had only the support of the Communist Party of Greece (KKE) and of the largest Greek anti-Nazi resistance organization (ELAS). The victory of the government anti-Communist forces led to Greece's membership in NATO and helped define the balance of ideological power in the region during the Cold War.

[4] Grigoris Lambrakis (1912-1963) was elected to Greek Parliament in 1961 as a candidate of the Pan-democratic Agrarian Movement of Greece on the ticket of the United Democratic Left (EDA). While not a Communist, Lambrakis's political views and ideology did lean towards the left, and was actively involved in the Pacifist Movement of his time. Using his Parliamentary immunity, in 1963 he marched in the banned walk for peace, from Marathon to central Athens. It was this march brought him under the political spotlight, making him a hero of the left and an enemy of the right. On May 22, 1963, after delivering a keynote speech at a pacifist meeting in the northern port city of Thessaloniki, he was run down by a delivery truck driven by two far-right extremists. He died five days later, on May 27, from brain injuries. Some 500,000 people attended his funeral in Athens, which became a protest rally against the right-wing government.

[5] The Greek Junta (1967-1974). In April, 21, 1967, three senior army officers (Giorgos Papadopoulos, Grigoris Spandidakis, and Stylianos Patakos) instigated a successful coup, claiming that a Communist takeover of Greece was imminent. Constantinos Kollias was made prime minister, but the real power rested with the three army officers. Soon after Papadopoulos and Patakos resigned their army posts and became prime minister and deputy prime minister respectively. The junta ended in 1974, following a bloody uprising by college students in Athens a year earlier.

Movement, of which her father was a leading figure for the northern sector, and as a child she will have to live in poverty and under a continuous persecution.

Maria will be only 6 months old when her family will flee their home in Thassos in the middle of the night in order to avoid being arrested by the forces of Anton Tsaous[6], boarding on a small fishing trawler that would take them across to the port of Ierissos in Chalikidiki, northern Greece. She will spend several nights hiding in the mountains along with her parents and members of the Resistance Movement; she will see her father being imprisoned, tortured, and sent to exile several times. Her father will be the first torture victim that Maria will ever see. She was only nine years old when she visited him at a prison in the northern port city of Thessaloniki.

"I entered his cell and saw him after he had been tortured. The first torture victim I ever saw was my own father!" said Maria during an interview at her house in downtown Athens. She explained that her mother would take her and her younger sister and make frequent visits to her father as they feared that he might be executed. But, as she noted they were not always successful in seeing him as the prison guards had been instructed to prevent them from meeting him. One day, and after their protests had intensify, the guards allowed only the two young girls to meet with the father so that her mother would not see the signs of his torture.

"We entered his cell, which was about only 1 meter (3 feet) long, and I see my father having pulled his legs close to his chest, his armpits wounded from exposure to boiling hot eggs, and the soles of his feet wounded from beatings—phalanx," said Maria while flipping through a photo album with pictures of her father from the early years. "Back then I knew nothing about torture, but I recorded in my mind all that my eyes could see so I could describe them later to my mother and our lawyer."

Who knew then that years later she would find herself examining thousands more victims of torture from foreign countries as a medical director of the torture rehab center in Athens . . .

Maria's father will be arrested repeatedly and for his family the years of his exile will be harsh and filled with poverty. Later, her own political activities and the Communist history of her father will become the pretext for her own arrest. In 1967, just months after she graduated from medical school and while she was making plans for post-graduate studies abroad, the military seized power in the country after a coup. Maria will be arrested and will be sent to exile to Gyaros[7]—the infamous "prison-island"

---

[6]   Anton Tsaous (formally known as Antonis Fosteridis) was the commander of a guerrilla force that fought against the Bulgarian troops that were occupying northern Greece in the early 1940s, and whose right-wing forces later turned against the Communist-led resistance guerrillas of EAM-ELAS in a power struggle that led to a civil war.

[7]   The uninhabited island of Gyaros is located in northern Cyclades. The 23-square-kilometers island was a point of exile for leftist political dissidents from 1948 to 1974. At least 22,000 people were exiled there.

as it was widely known—the same place where her father had been exiled when she was still a little girl.

At the time of her arrest Maria was 23 years old and with a promising future. She had already made plans to do a specialization in endocrinology at a university abroad. But the military coup will come like a sun eclipse to cast a dark cloak over her dreams and to those of millions of other Greeks. Maria will be arrested at the port of Piraeus near Athens as she was trying to board a cruise ship for Australia, betrayed by a friend of hers who tipped off the security police about her plans.

Many years later she will manage to see her police file and to discover that authorities had started collecting information on her ever since she was little girl. "The first entry in my file was recorded when I was about 10 to 11 years old. It was when my father was returning from prison and he would send me to get a newspaper. The charge stated: 'She would walk toward the kiosk and buy the newspaper, but instead of delivering it immediately to her father she would sit at the stairway and read it to the last page.' This was the first charge in my police file," she noted.

Maria will spend about one year in exile on the prison-island of Gyaros, from where she will leave only after being diagnosed with an internal hemorrhage and cardiac insufficiency (the medical term for a weak heart). The junta didn't want to be credited with Maria's death so she will be taken to a hospital to the nearby island of Syros, where the doctors will call for her immediate transfer to a hospital in Athens as she needed to undergo urgent surgery. There, Maria will come closer to death that ever in her life.

During her exile on Gyaros, Maria will use her medical degree to get a position at the infirmary, from where she will help many exiles who were considering signing a statement of obedience to leave Gyaros on a medical emergency. That way Maria would give them a unique opportunity to think with a clear mind and decide on their own—away from the influence of the communist party—if they truly want to sign a statement of obedience with the junta and return home to their families. As Maria notes, some of those who left on her advised 'medical emergency' would never return to Gyaros, choosing to sign the statement of obedience and save their marriage even if it meant getting on the Communist Party's black list. Those people, according to Maria, were heroes as they had the courage to choose living the rest of their lives with the stigma of the traitor that the Communist Party would attach to their names—the same party for which they suffered relentless persecution and even harsh exile—just because they wanted to save their marriage. But their brave act was never acknowledged and their names were never printed in any newspaper, remaining shadows of heroes like Ayiad.

In Gyaros, Maria will also come face-to-face with the dictator Stylianos Patakos[8] during his visit to the prison-island along with two U.S. senators—the names of which she never found out. Maria will have a short conversation with the dictator, while she will disrupt the program of the U.S. senators by revealing to them the shocking reality that the prison did not only house men—as they had been told—but also hundreds of women. As Maria noted, publicly the junta was very tight-lipped about the number of exiles who were sent to Gyaros, while at times it was even denying their very existence. It was those denials that prompted a German magazine to rent a small plane and send a photographer to prove the existence of those exiles. Maria notes that one of the photos published in the magazine showed in the backyard waiving a cloth in the air.

"At some point Patakos turns around and tells me: 'Hear this little girl. One day you will leave this place because you love people . . . This is how I started as well and look what I have become, a dictator!'" Maria said about her meeting with Patakos on Gyaros.

The first years after the exile will also be particularly harsh. The first two years she will have to remain at house arrest, while she will have to report to the local police station once a week. Her political identity will also become the reason for losing her job at several hospitals where she was trying to complete her specialization. Her dismissals were always ordered by the boards of obedience that the junta had established in all state institutions, including hospitals. It would take her eight years to complete her specialization.

The Greek junta—just like the regime of Saddam Hussein later, and other authoritarian regimes—will leave hundreds of torture victims behind it, as an open social wound to remind future generation of its barbarity.

Cases of torture and ill-treatment of people who resisted the junta had been documented in newspapers of the time as well as in books that were written later by former exiles, but until recently no one knew if this "social wound" had finally heal.

An effort to provide an answer to this grim question came a few years ago when a seven-member team of the Medical Rehabilitation Center for Torture Victims (MRCT) in Athens—including Maria who was the medical director of the center—tried to conduct a research study about it. The difficulties[9] they faced in carrying out the

---

[8]   Brigadier Stylianos Patakos was one of the three senior army officers who instigated the military coup in Greece in 1967. Soon after the army took over control of the country Patakos resigned from his army post and became deputy prime minister, a post he held for the duration of the junta.

[9]   Out of the 23 torture victims that the medical rehab center contacted, eight of them refused to participate in the study by arguing that all those years they had found comfort in their silence, trying to erase from their memory those days of horror. Of the 15 victims

study was a clear sign that the "wound" was still open and the pain in the psyche of the victims was still fresh even though some 25 had elapsed since the restoration of democracy in the country.

Using a list of names that the team had compile from newspaper clips of the time and from various other documents, they started contacting the torture victims by mail and later by phone, asking them for their participation in the study. Of the 10 victims—seven men and three women—who finally agreed to participate in the study, the team of experts concluded that some of them were still suffering from psychopathological symptoms even after all these years since their torture. Out of those who participated in the study, two had been arrested once; four had been arrested twice; two had been arrested three times; two others had been arrested as many as four times; three had been jailed at least once while someone else twice. The mean time of detention was 69 months, with the minimum time being one month and the maximum 236 months. At the same time mean time of imprisonment was 45 months, with the minimum time being 30 months and the maximum 60 months. According to the study, aside from the physical injuries that were sustained during the incarceration at the detention centers of military police and various prisons, some of the victims exhibited a series of psychopathological symptoms[10] even after all those years.

Although the sample of the study is relatively small to reach any scientific conclusions, the findings offer a small but very gruesome glimpse of the wounds that the torturers of the junta inflicted on the bodies of their victims, as well as to their tormented souls. According to studies, the Greek junta used as many as 22 torture methods[11].

"The torture was used as a measure for quelling any form of resistance, forcing an entire nation to be 'placed in a cast'—as the paranoid dictator used to say. The 'cast' means the suspension of all principles, traditions, and of ideals like democracy, freedom, and justice which are deeply-rooted in the past of the Greek people, and

---

who initially agreed to participate in the study, three never showed up in their sessions and two had no further contact with the medical center. Those who refused participation provided various excuses: two said that they had no spare time; one felt that the experience would aggravate him; two said they were not interested; while another said that the issue is highly personal and expressed concerns over the confidentiality of medical records.

[10]   One of the victims during the torture session had exhibited reactive psychosis while during the examination he did not show any signs of psychopathology. The diagnosis in another victim revealed a multiple-substance abuse, while another victim exhibited symptoms of panic disorder. Finally, one of the victims was diagnosed with compulsive disorder, while another in the past suffered from an acute depression disorder.

[11]   The torture methods included sexual abuse and rape; Psychological pressure; electroshock to various parts of the body; and phalanx (beating on the sole of the feet).

which accompanied them all those years of occupation and helped them maintain their identity," said Maria.

She noted that the junta used two types of torture. "In the period 1967-1974 the junta employed the use of torture for two purposes: to extract information related to the activities of the resistance and the quelling of political activities by citizens," said Maria. "The acts of torture were carried out by trained middle-ranking officers from the police, navy and army police—which was also known by its acronym (ESA). The strategy used in their torture methodology instructed them not to leave any visible marks on the bodies of their victims, or to prevent any visitations until the marks are gone. But over the years the purposes for the use of torture changed and during the period 1971-1974 the junta used torture as means to coerce and terrorize the detainee or prisoner, serving that way its ultimate goal of crushing the student movement. During that period it was reservists of military police who carried most of the acts of torture, and who were encouraged by their superiors to leave marks and scars on the bodies of their victims. Over those years the military police conducted random arrests and detentions, subjecting those people to ill-treatment and torture and who soon after were released without ever being charged with anything."

But, although the seven years of the junta left behind widespread scars and marks, the Greek society seemed to turn page in its book of history faster than other societies that had experiences tyrannical regimes. According to Maria, a major factor in this successful healing process is Greece's unique example where soon after the fall of the junta its leaders and torturers were tried and sent to jail.

Indeed, over 400 torturers were tried, convicted, and imprisoned for the ill-treatment and torture of thousands of Greeks during the junta. Furthermore, a few years after the restoration of democracy Greece passed a law prohibiting the use of torture, and which would be enacted before the 1984 international Convention Against Torture and Other Cruel, Inhuman or Degrading Treatment or Punishment of that Greece also ratified.

WITHOUT MERCY

The atmosphere in the room of the Medical Rehabilitation Center for Torture Victims in Balayayo, Zimbabwe, is pretty tense. In the middle of the room sits a man, his wife and their child—a small boy that moves nervously his little legs as he sits on his mother's lap and looks around the room with fear in his eyes. His father, a tall black man in his 40s, sits in an armchair with his right arm and left leg in a cast. His wife looks at their young boy and an expression of pain and distress takes over her facial expressions as her husband starts talking to two doctors who are sitting across from them. The doctors, both member of the International Rehabilitation Council for Torture Victims[12], were Inge Genefke and Maria—who was president of the council at the time.

"I heard a thunderous knock on the door of the house and someone asked: 'is anyone here?'" the man said, referring to a recent incident on the night of May 13, 2000 when about 20 armed men came to his house. But the voice coming from behind the door sounded familiar to him, so when he opened the door he saw his neighbor—who was a war veteran—along with some 20 men armed with axes, iron rods, and guns.

"As soon as I saw that a large number of men were at the doorstep I started to retreat and then they started to break down the door with the axes," he said while looking at his son who was nervously chewing an apple. As he explained, moments later the armed men were inside his home, threatening to harm his family and saying that they would burn down the building.

"I told them: 'Take my wife and child outside and then you can kill me,'" he added, noting that his wish was granted and his family was soon outside in the front yard.

---

[12]   The International Rehabilitation Council for Torture Victims (*www.irct.org*) is an independent, international health professional organization that promotes and supports the rehabilitation of torture victims and works for the prevention of torture worldwide. Based in Copenhagen, Denmark, the IRCT has a network of nearly 200 rehabilitation centers worldwide. The council, established in 1985, has special consultative status with the UN Economic and Social Council and the UN Department of Public Information, and participatory status with the Council of Europe—the human rights watchdog of the European Union.

"After they were taken outside one of the men told me: 'now you can go outside as well so we can search the house without anyone in here,'" he told the doctors, explaining that this was an excuse so they could search for membership cards of MDC (Movement for Democratic Change), of which he was a member. "As soon as I walked outside they started to beat me," he said as one of the doctors asked him as to how many men were involved in his beating. Gazing at ceiling and with an expression of doubt sketched on his face he told them: "I cannot say for sure, but they had surrounded me. You see they had me lay face down before they started to hit me. Then one of them raised his axe and started to strike at my leg, trying to cut it off."

After a while, and as they were still beating him and threatening to harm his family, they dragged him some 200 meters (650 feet) away from his home. There they unleashed their entire wrath against him, hitting him on the chest and head for about three hours until he was unconscious and then they left him there to bleed to death.

The man, whose name is not mentioned here to protect his identity, after a few days found out that a neighbor of his had named him as a member of the opposition party.

As the man was telling the doctors about the night of the attack, his wife was sitting in a chair beside him with a vacant look in her eyes and their little boy on her lap until it was her turn to tell the doctors that she was also the victim of a beating that night—something that her husband was unaware until they woke up next to each other in the hospital.

She told the doctors that the men used crowbars and fists to beat her repeatedly on the chest under the breasts, while her child saw the entire incident as she was carrying it on her back the whole time.

Maria, who was participating in the mission of the non-governmental organizations as president of IRCT, listened carefully to the stories of the victims while she was consulting their medical records. The diagnosis in both cases confirmed the stories of the victims. In the man's case, the diagnosis—aside from the physical injuries that were verified—the medical anti-torture team also found that he exhibited depression symptoms and he was emotionally vulnerable. His wife, who witnessed part of her husband's torture, exhibited depression symptoms, anxiety and distress. The third diagnosis involved the little boy, which was only four years old, and which perhaps was the most tragic case in the story. According to the diagnosis, two days after the attack the boy was still in a state of shock, spending most of the time in his mother's arms and not saying a word. Ever since the attack he has said nothing about the incident and he has rejected his father—with whom until the day of the attack he had a very close relationship—showing strong signs of anger towards him.

Soon after the young couple had cleared the room, a man walked into the room, the second case of the day. In his mid-30s and wearing a black jacket, dark blue shirt and gray pants, the dark-skin man greeted the doctors by bowing to them and then proceeded to the empty chair in the middle of the room. In contrast with the previous victims that the doctors had just examined—who had visible signs from a physical attack—this man appeared to be in good health. All they could observe as he was sitting before them was the expressions of pain and anger that were sketched all over his face. Nothing prepared them for what they were about to hear.

"It was around 7 o'clock in the afternoon of that day when they came to my house from all directions on trucks," he said while gesturing with his hands—a clear sign of his tenseness. "There were three teams, one came into the house from the back door, the other from the front entrance and the third from the sides. They all came in at the same time. At the time my wife and my children were sitting in the living room watching TV. The first thing that the intruders did was to smash the television set and then they started destroying everything! Everything! Everything!" he said and the anger started to take over all of his gestures and body movements, which were becoming more jumpy as he was telling the story.

"Then they started hitting my family and asking them to tell them where I was," he said while noting that at the time of the incident he was not at home. "When they didn't get the answers they were looking for they started to hit them with crowbars and bludgeons. As they were beating them, one of them turns to my 20-year-old son and tells him: 'You, come here,' and then my son made two steps forward. Then they grabbed a cement block that they had found in the front yard and threw it with force on his chest, knocking him on the ground. As he was lying on the ground, they attacked him with axes and blew two deep wounds on his head. Right after, and while my son was lying on the ground in a pool of his own blood, they started throwing rocks all over his body," the man said as his anger had grown to rage and his pain unbearable.

"At the same time the others continued to attack the rest of my family and trashing my house, demanding to tell them where I was. Then my wife told them that they rather killed her than her children, but that enraged them even more and then they started to hit her on the face and stomach. As she had folded in pain they kept asking her about me. One of them wanted to continue her beating but someone else ordered him to stop, and they did. It was then that she got up and run to the kitchen and from there she run out of the house. The children managed to follow her after receiving some more beatings from the intruders," he said as he paused to take a deep breath before continuing, while the doctors kept detailed notes.

"But my older son was still inside the house and soon they doused him with gasoline to burn him alive. Then one of them said: 'since we will burn down the house he will die in the fire.' So, they locked the house and started a fire with my son bleeding on the floor inside. At the end he managed to get out the house before the roof collapsed," he said, stressing that his son's transfer to the hospital was delayed greatly because the authorities did not arrive at the scene right away.

As he explained to the doctors, his only wrongdoing for which his entire family was traumatized and his house destroyed was being a member of MDC, the main opposition party.

A sudden silence covered the room for a moment as the young man walked out, but it was soon broken as another man who was about 10 years younger took his place. With his eyes lowered and a serious expression on his face, the young man started to unfold his own story of torture by the war veterans—the thugs of the ruling party.

As he explained, it was on the afternoon of May 24 and he was at the local offices of MDC along with a friend preparing for an upcoming protest rally when a group of 20 to 30 men—which he said were war veterans—stormed the building and rounded them up in the street. There they forced them to undress and lay down on their stomachs, kicking them and hitting them with bludgeons on the head and body. The attack lasted about one hour, during which they broke several of his ribs, put out cigarettes on various parts of his body, and beat him on the soles of his feet (phalanx). During his torture his attackers accused him and the party he supported for selling out the country to the white people, while they threatened to kill him if he didn't give up the names of other MDC supporters.

After he finished recounting his attack the young man lowered his shirt so the doctors could start the examination, while Maria had already started walking towards him. "Atrophied scar from a blow and a linear scar from a knife," she said while pointing to different parts of his face. "Scars from cigarette burns on his neck. Abrasion on his left shoulder. Scar from a blow with a bludgeon on his back. Scars from cigarette burns. All of these show that the torture was systematic. Also, there is a large abrasion near the kidney. Moreover, as we saw in the x-rays there is a fracture in the lower jaw," said Maria as she was finishing the examination of the young man—the third of 10 cases that they reviewed that day.

It was the summer of 2000 and Zimbabwe—this former British colony that was known as Rhodesia[13] in southern Africa—was two months away from national elections and its people appeared to be hostage of organized violence by supporters of the Zimbabwe African National Union-Patriotic Front (ZANU PF), the ruling socialist party of President Robert Mugabe.

"It all started two months ago when President Mugabe held a referendum for the seizing of land that belonged to whites," Maria noted during a meeting with reporters in Athens. "But the people responded with a thunderous 'NO' and then he decided to mobilize the war veterans, warning them that if the opposition party came to power then the country would lose its independence."

---

[13] The United Kingdom annexed Southern Rhodesia from the South Africa Company in 1923. A 1961 constitution was formulated that favored whites in power. In 1965 the government unilaterally declared its independence, but the UK did not recognize the act and demanded more complete voting rights for the Black African majority in the country (then called Rhodesia). UN sanctions and guerilla uprising finally to free elections in 1979 and independence (as Zimbabwe).

The message was received and according to data from human rights organizations over 5,000 people—in their vast majority ordinary people—fell victims to the organized political violence, which would last for more than two years, while over 80 people would lose their life in politically-motivated attacks in May 2000.

Mugabe, a former teacher who was raised and educated as a Roman-Catholic, became a committed Marxist during the guerilla war against the Rhodesian Front government of Ian Smith. He came into the political spotlight after leading the country to independence in 1980, but he soon turned into an authoritarian leader who has been ruling the country for over 25 years[14] by enforcing strict control over the media and the rights of its people.

According to a study by the IRCT, in Zimbabwe—a country where homosexuality is punished by law with a prison sentence of up to 10 years—the political violence with the beatings, torture and humiliation of people has emerged as large-scale psychological torture that spread throughout the country, making people to feel helpless and to suffer from constant psychological distress.

"What is very important to mention is that in these attacks the acts of violence are not carried out by police officers or the military, as it is customary around the world, but ordinary people—including women—who are simply supporters of the ruling political party," said Maria while presenting her findings[15] to a group of diplomats from the European Union, the United States, Canada, Australia and New Zealand in Harare. "What we should also note," she told the diplomats, "is that the psychological violence, threats and even the destruction of property, is a powerful weapon against powerless people. The psychological torture of this kind is widespread and its power to make an entire society to silence has been underestimated."

Maria explained that it was impossible to accurately map the true impact of the mass psychological violence, but she noted that based on similar prior cases the true extend of its impact becomes clearly visible only after the lapse of several years and it is usually triggers long-term societal and political consequences.

"We are afraid that violence will grow to uncontainable proportions since anyone wearing a T-shirt with the logo of an opposition party is a target," Maria said.

---

[14]   Robert Mugabe came to power in 1980, as soon as the country gained its independence from British rule. A founder of the Zimbabwe African National Union-Patriotic Front (ZANU PF) party, he served as prime minister from April 18, 1980 to Dec. 31, 1987, and as president from Dec. 31, 1987 until today.

[15]   According to the findings, the torture was systematic and, among others, included beatings, hanging from the wrists, extinguishing cigarettes on various parts of the body, electroshock, mock executions, death threats and psychological torture. Moreover, the office of a renowned doctor—who was also the leader of war veterans in the upcoming elections—had become a torture center.

Indeed, the violence that started that summer was only the beginning. Ordinary people—the majority of them blue-collar workers—would fall victims of politically-motivated violence. The violent attacks, torture, rapes, disappearances and executions of ordinary will soon gain epidemic proportions and an entire nation of 12 million people will fall ill—physically and psychologically.

The violence will continue[16] until the presidential elections of 2002. The party of Robert Mugabe will win the elections—as it did for over 20 years—in spite the strong criticism over the validity of the results by the international community and the foreign observers in the country.

The now overt violations of human rights by the government of Robert Mugabe would force the European Union to consider freezing funds[17] of aid to Zimbabwe, to bar members of the Zimbabwean government from traveling to the European Union, and to freeze all assets that the Zimbabwean government had in European banks. This move by the European Union, which aimed at discouraging President Mugabe from continuing his oppressive tactics against his people by threatening to cut a much-need aid to his poor country, had exactly the opposite effect. Mugabe expanded his intimidation and oppression tactics to include the international non-governmental human rights organizations that were in his country.

That year one of the human rights groups that became a target of Mugabe's regime was Amani Trust—the same torture rehabilitation center that two years before had invited Amnesty International and the IRCT to Zimbabwe in order to examine and record cases of violence by supporters of the ruling party. For weeks government-controlled newspapers would print commentaries and editorials critical of Amani Trust—the flagship among rights group in the recording[18] of human rights violations in Zimbabwe and in the treatment of torture victims—in order to smear its image.

As time passed the newspaper reports against Amani Trust increased, as did the pressure by the government of Robert Mugabe, with police officers making frequent unannounced inspections at the office's of the organization and even the homes of its employees. Some of the employees said that they were even ordered to appear

---

[16]   According to non-governmental organizations, over 1,000 cases of torture were recorded in 2002 while more than 60 people lost their life in politically-motivated attacks.

[17]   In 2002 the European Union threatened the government of Robert Mugabe with freezing and aid of 128 million Euros for the period 2002-2007. The previous two years the European Union had already started to reduce the aid it was fueling into Zimbabwe from 30 million Euros to 5 million.

[18]   According to records from the Amani Trust, at least 50 people lost their life in politically-motivated attacks by supporters of the ruling party in the months leading up to the 2002 elections, while more than 20,000 were forced to flee their homes due to the violence.

regularly at local police stations. It was clear that Mugabe aimed at forcing out of Zimbabwe any foreign presence that threatened the viability of his regime, isolating that way his country even more.

"We are attempting to get some comment from the police as to why they are doing this, but so far we have been unable to get any understanding as to why we are getting this kind of attention," Anthony Reeler, director of Amani Trust, said in an interview with the Financial Gazette in Harare on May 23, 2002. According to Reeler, two weeks ago Home Affair Minister John Nkomo had warned that the government would crack down on non-governmental organizations involved in "subversive activities" and were "actively involved in undermining the nation's internal security."

"I don't know why the government would want to do that because we have no political position," Reeler, a psychology professor, had explained then. "We deal with human rights issues, irrespective of who is involved. In the statements that we issue, we have said the government is not doing enough to prevent human rights violations and we will continue to say that if we feel enough is not being done."

Soon the articles in the government-controlled newspapers will become even more aggressive and one of them particularly will alarm Reeler as well as Maria who then was still president of IRCT.

"According to an article in the government-controlled Herald that is based on false claims, the medical rehabilitation center of victims of violence in Zimbabwe, known as Amani Trust, has been under persecution and its employees are in danger because—according to the claims of the newspaper—the center has rented homes which it calls 'safe houses' and gives them to people who take part in protest rallies against President Mugabe, and that it pays each person $200 to take part in attacks against supporters of the ruling party," Maria wrote in a protest letter that she sent out following the provocative newspaper report, as Amani Trust is one of the 200 centers under IRCT.

Another newspaper, the Mail on Sunday, wrote in January 2002 that Reeler and his organization are "accomplices in acts of terror and mayhem that being perpetrated by MDC killer cells."

"The allegations by the government papers against Anthony Reeler and the Amani Trust are false and baseless, and they are trying to turn the victimizer Mugabe into a victim," Maria noted. "I want to stress my grave concern about the safety of professor Anthony Reeler and of the staff of Amani Trust, who continue to provide medical and legal assistance to the victims in a country where basic human rights continue to be violated."

The letter, which aimed sensitizing the international media and launch an international campaign to protect the staff of the local anti-torture center in Harare, would proven powerless in preventing the government security forces from raiding the medical center, attacking the staff, and seizing the computers and medical files of torture victims.

Reeler was now a fugitive on the run hiding from the government security forces while the medical rehab center was shut down, leaving out in the street hundreds of torture victims.

The same period that Mugabe's security forces would shut down the offices of Amani Trust, relations between Washington and Harare will be strained over a beating by ZANU-PF supporters of a U.S. embassy worker who was trying to carry out a study into the effects of Mugabe's controversial land redistribution scheme.

According to Reeler, his organization was targeted by Mugabe's regime because during that period they were collecting information in order to compile new reports about human rights violations in the country, and which if they were published it would further harm Zimbabwe's image abroad.

With a coordinated effort by the IRCT and others in Harare, Reeler would finally manage to flee the country. Mugabe had finally succeeded and now he could continue his campaign of torture without any monitoring.

In April 2005 the ZANU-PF party will once again win the elections and the 81-year-old Mugabe will win 2/3 of the parliament seats, giving him the legislative power to tailor the constitution to his wishes. The international community once again criticized the elections of being rigged by violence, while two British journalists working for the London-based Sunday Telegraph were arrested, tried and deported for covering the elections without a permit.

But, perhaps the most tragic event of all came in April 2005 when Zimbabwe—a country with such a bloody human rights record—was reelected to the U.N.'s main human rights body, the Human Rights Commission. Zimbabwe will hold this position for the next three years . . .

IN THE SHADOWS OF SOUTH LEBANON

It was the summer of 2003 and Maria was once again packing her bags for one more trip abroad. This time her destination was Lebanon, a country that even today has visible scars from the wounds left behind from the 16 years of civil war and partial occupation by Israel.

Lebanon—a country that gained its independence from the European colonialists in 1944—will repeatedly[19] come to war with neighboring Israel. The government of Israel will accuse Beirut time and time again of not doing enough to control the activities[20] of Palestinian rebels who had found shelter in the country, and in 1968 the Israeli forces will start a series of counterattacks aimed at the Palestinian guerilla forces within Lebanon.

In a last-ditch effort to disengage itself from the fighting between Israel and the Palestinian militant groups operating on its soil and to show a neutral stance, the government of Lebanon will decide against its involvement in the great Arab-Israeli war that will break out in October 1973. But it will also refrain from exercising any control over the activities of the Palestinian groups in South Lebanon.

Two years later, in 1975, Lebanon will be embroiled in a civil war between Christians, Muslims and Palestinian militant groups, which with the 'help' of Israel and Syria will last as many as 16 years, leaving tens of thousands of Lebanese dead and an economy in ruins. The Israeli army—which from the beginning of the conflict

---

[19] As a member of the Arab League, Lebanon declared war on Israel in 1948 but took little part in the conflict. During the 1967 Arab-Israeli War, Lebanon gave verbal support to the Arab effort against Israel but did not become involved in any military action.

[20] In 1969 fighting broke out between the Lebanese army and the Palestinian militants after the government had threatened to limit the latter's activities. Following the bloody suppression in the 1970-71 of the Palestinian guerillas in Jordan, large numbers of Palestinians fled into South Lebanon and Beirut, opening a larger front for the Lebanese government who was trying to curb their activities.

would side with the Christians of Lebanon—in the course of the civil war will invade Lebanon twice[21].

The cooperation of the Israeli Defense Force (known by its acronym as IDF) with the Christian fighters of the South Lebanese Army (also known as SLA) will last for years, even after the partial withdrawal of the Israeli forces from Lebanon in 1985. Israel will pull out its remaining forces from Lebanon in the spring of 2000. A U.N. peacekeeping force numbering some 2,000 troops now patrols the U.N.-drawn boundary, or Blue Line, between South Lebanon and Israel.

During the civil war the concentration camps of the SLA in the southern areas of Lebanon will become known as "Hellish," spreading the terror across the country for years.

Lebanon was not a strange land to Maria—who also was very aware of its history—since it was the third time she was visiting the Middle-Eastern country. This time the reason for the trip was a conference on torture, which was being organized in the capital of Lebanon on June 26th—a day that the United Nations have declared it as an International Day in Support of Victims of Torture.

"This conference is the scream that breaks that silence that covers torture and calls for its eradication and the conviction of the torturers," said Mohammed Safa, the slim secretary general of the Khiam Rehabilitation Center for Victims of Torture (KRC). Khiam, a rural area in South Lebanon, entered the international spotlight during the years of the civil war when unspeakable acts of torture were carried out in a prison camp that was operated by the SLA.

Addressing an audience of human rights defenders from the Arab world and Europe who had gathered at the U.N. offices in Beirut, Safa said: "Here in Arabia we are people who have suffered the worst torture and violations of human rights, such as the Israeli occupation and the inhumane violations in Palestine and South Lebanon, but also by the tyrannical Arab systems which if it was possible they would have prohibited they people to speak."

---

[21]   The first time that Israel invaded Lebanon was March 1978 when in response to attacks by Palestinian militants of the Palestine Liberation Organization (PLO) it deployed a 20,00-strong force into South Lebanon—an area it occupied for the next four months—and creating that way a "security zone" that extended several miles deep into Lebanon. Under pressure from the U.N. Security Council, Israel withdrew its forces from the territory, but transferred control to the pro-Israeli Christian militias, the South Lebanon Army (SLA). The second invasion—and the fiercest one—came on June 6, 1982 when the Israeli army marched to west of Beirut and trapped some 6,000 Palestinian fighters in the southwest of the country. As a result, some 7,000 Palestinians were forced to leave Lebanon under the supervision of a Multinational Force comprised of U.S. and European-allied troops, who left immediately afterward.

On the third day of the conference—which included testimonies of torture victims and ex-detainees—Safa escorted the delegates to torture place in South Lebanon, including the place of his martyrdom. The three Israeli ex-prisons visited were Ansar, Khiam, and Tal Al-Nhass.

"On the last day we made a visit to South Lebanon, starting from a detention camp where Mohammed Safa—the founder and the psyche of this initiative—was detained," said Maria during an interview in Athens after she returned from Lebanon. "This man was held for 10 months in this prison and during our visit there he described the torture he was subjected to." Maria noted that thousands of Lebanese people were tortured in those camps over a period of 20 years.

"Even our bus driver was a torture victim himself," she said while shifting her body towards the reporter as an effort to emphasize her shock. "All those people who were released from that prison camp they were all victims of torture. Of course when we visited the place a large section of the camp was destroyed as they had been demolished in an effort to get rid of any evidence."

The second visit was to the Khiam Detention Center (KDC), which was also located near the Golan Heights and the border with Israel. There, behind the tall white walls that in the past were guarded by armed guards of the South Lebanon Army (SLA), a story of horror was written for thousands[22] of Lebanese people.

"This prison camp was the site of really horrible acts of torture, where the use of electricity—meaning electroshock—was the prime torture method they used," said Maria as her face started to wrinkle with pain.

Safa said that based on eyewitness accounts as many as 143 Lebanese detainees were released on May 23, 2000, the day that the Khiam prison camp was officially closed.

The torture that was carried out at the Khiam prison camp were so horrific and cruel that at least 14 people died during interrogation, while three more died in the hospital after their release. The youngest prisoner at the camp was 14-years-old and the oldest 83-years-old—and who was detained for as many as seven months. Some of the prisoners were held as many as 15 years at the Khiam camp.

"I bought the books for the school year that was about to begin," said Kamil, a high school student, about the day that his life changed forever. "But on the same night, I woke up by a loud voice. It was my father shouting, "There is nobody in this room. The Israelis did not allow me to change my night garment. They took me and I spent the first night in a room full of mice. I was taken in the morning to the Khiam camp. I was ordered to stand there near a wall until late at night. I was then

---

[22]   According to official reports, over 5,000 Lebanese citizens were imprisoned in the Khiam prison camp between 1985 and 2000—the year that the Israeli troops made their final withdrawal from South Lebanon.

taken to a room and a person started questioning me. I told him I was student. So he asked me, 'Do you know what this is?' I tried to touch it since I was blindfolded. It turned out to be a scourge made by a collection of electric wires. He ordered me to kneel down and started whipping my back and my bare feet for three hours until I fell helplessly on the ground. After dragging me and tying me to a post, he started throwing cold and hot water on my naked body. I was then put in a solitary confinement that had no access to the sun for one week. During the second session of torture, the interrogators wrapped a metallic wire between my fingers, ordered me to kneel down and spilled water on my body. As I felt the electric current flowing to my blood, my whole body started shaking uncontrollably. They put the electric wire on my genitals and between my teeth. Each day carried a new way of torture with it. The interrogator whose weight was over 100 kilograms had walked over my back. He once hit me hard with a rough stick on my head that my sight was weakened. Whenever I asked to see a doctor, their answer was 'We have no doctors here.' I threatened them of doing a hunger strike to death. So, an Israeli doctor examined my eyes and said there was no treatment for my eyes. He added that he would give me a walking stick because I was going to lose my sight in a short period as he said."

Kamil was released on December 1991 after spending two years in the Khiam prison camp. But his life had changed forever as the torture he was subjected to left irreparable damage to his body.

"I tried to go back to school following my release but was unable to read or see what was written on the board. I couldn't continue my education," Kamil said in a testimony he offered to the Khiam Rehabilitation Center for Victims of Torture[23].

But Kamil will not be the only young student who will be imprisoned and tortured at the Khiam prison camp. Rabah will be arrested in front of the terrorized eyes of his schoolmates and he will be detained at the Khiam prison camp for little over one year.

"I was detained from my school in the village of Kfar Shouba," Rabah said in his testimony to the Khiam rehab center about the events of March 23, 1998. "SLA members entered the classroom and asked me to go with them. I was only 13 years old. They took me to the Khiam camp where I had to stay in a cell that was one meter (3 feet) long and half a meter wide during the interrogation period which lasted for one month and the half. They used to interrogate me late at night, usually with my hands chained and a sack on my head. They applied electricity on my fingers, my tongue and other sensitive areas of the body. I used to faint. But the interrogator

---

[23]   The Khiam Rehabilitation Center for Victims of Torture was established in 1999 and has its headquarters in Beirut. Its primary objective is "to register and count the health and psychological conditions of the persons who have rescued from the Israeli concentration camps of torture," and "establish centers for medical, psychological and physical treatment and social, professional and educational rehabilitation.

would wake me up by throwing me with cold water. He would wait for 10 minutes before throwing hot water on me. The interrogator used to say to me after the interrogation session was finished: 'We were not tough on you because you're very young.' During my detention, my mother and two sisters were also held in the camp. When I was released, the military official there said: 'We are releasing you because of your young age and your sickness.' I was suffering from fractures in my thoracic cavity that was resulted from kicking. I was expelled after my release with other members of my family. My sisters and my mother were also expelled from our village after their release."

Rabah was released from the Khiam prison camp on May 16, 1989.

In their testimonies Kamil and Rabah confirm that electroshock was one of the principal methods of torture used by the torturers of the SLA and the Israelis at the Khiam prison camp, as well as the different uses of electroshock in the teeth, the fingers and the genitalia. Other methods used at the Khiam camp included the phalanx—the beating with wooden or metallic objects at the sole of the feet—as well as the use of cold and hot water. According to experts who are involved in the treatment of torture victims, the torture methods employed by the SLA provide a clear indication that the torturers had undergo training in torture techniques. Some even say that they had been trained by the Israeli army, who controlled the area of the South Lebanon with the assistance of the SLA.

One case, though, that of Hussein who was detained at the Khiam prison camp for two years at the end of 1980s, indicates that the torturers of SLA also experimented on other forms of torture which were equally cruel and horrifying.

"I was kidnapped from my house in Taybe and taken to the Khiam Detention Center," said Hussein in his testimony to the Khiam rehab center about the events of April 4, 1987.

"They put me in the outdoors for the first 3 days kicking and beating me all up. I was whipped on my back and feet with iron chains and hung on the pole for 2 days, and then I was put to a hen house. Various types of torture were inflicted on us; my nails were taken out, slowly and painfully, and I have seen them taking Jamal's nails out with a wrench and N. H.'s hair with pincers. Electrification was inflicted on our fingers and feet, as well as on the tongues and genital areas and they put out cigarettes on our chest. We were allowed a bath every 3 months. As for the humiliation where one can feel he/she are not human beings anymore, this is what they do best; we had to stand up for any soldier who was passing by, while one of the Israeli soldiers spilled coffee on his shoes and told me to lick it. I was hit in my rectum when I was stripped naked and they put a handy bomb in the rectum of another detainee to force him to confess. Malnutrition was terrible, and the thirst was even worse . . . one drank his own urine because he hadn't had any drink of liquid for weeks . . ."

Hussein was released in the winter of 1989, after spending two horrendous years in the hands of the SLA torturers at the Khiam prison camp.

Moreover, according to Maria, the torturers of Khiam did not limit their gruesome torture methods to male detainees, but they also used them during their notorious interrogations of young women. Maria actually spoke with one of them in a meeting she had with Hezbollah[24] officials, in which they negotiated for access to areas of South Lebanon near the Israeli border for the delegates.

"This woman came and pulled me on the side and in private she told me: 'Now you will go to see the place where torture was carried out, but no woman there is going to tell you what she went through. When we were menstruating they would take us for electroshock because during that time the spasms are even greater, and ever since none of us could have children," said Maria as she was describing her meeting with one of the female torture victims of Lebanon.

With just those few words that woman managed to offer a grim glimpse into the horror that those women had suffered in the hands of the SLA torturers. Other women were not as graphic in their torture stories they offered to the Khiam rehab center.

One of them was Sonia, who was imprisoned at the Khiam Detention Center (KDC) on Feb. 25, 1991 and was released three years later on Aug. 3, 1994.

"It all started when they decided to make my brother to be forcefully enrolled in the pro-Israeli militias," she said in her testimony. "They surrounded the house and took me, with a bag over my head so that I couldn't see anything, and put me to a dark room in spite of all my screaming. One of the soldiers came to me and said that my brother confessed about me. I did not say anything, so he said that he was going to put me in a room full of men who would take turns in raping me, it was then that I had a nervous breakdown. The next day, they whipped my feet until I fainted. They made me kneel down for a whole hour and asked me to work for them, when I refused they re-started to beat me up and insult me. I was put to 3 months solitary room with hot and cold water being daily thrown at me. I refused to work with them and told them that I would rather stay imprisoned for 20 years than to deal with them. During the time my brother and I were in the KDC, my father died. He had a breakdown and died because he knew what the KDC meant".

After concluding their tour of the area of the Khiam prison camp, Maria and the other delegates later in the evening wrapped-up the three-day conference with a visit to the Kfar-Hamam village in South Lebanon near the Israeli border. There, Maria inaugurated the "House of Lebanese Detainee," a small rehabilitation center which was created with the support of the International Rehabilitation Council for Torture Victims (IRCT)—of which Maria was president at the time—and the Khiam Rehabilitation Center for Victims of Torture.

---

[24] Hezbollah, a Shiite organization, gained inspiration and training in the 1980s from Iran and continues to receive backing from the clerical regime in Tehran. The United States lists Hezbollah as a terrorist group.

"We arrive at the village and we see the children gathered at the main square and wearing the white T-shirts with the logo 'Together Against Torture,'" said Maria. "The village—which by the way it was Communistic and featured the hammer and sickle emblem—was the only one which was not controlled by the Hezbollah."

But as she noted, the most intriguing discovery was that almost all of those who lived at the Kfar-Hamam village were victims of torture. "It was something incredible. It got to the point where I asked: 'Isn't anyone here who is not a victim of torture?'" Maria noted, stressing that even the delegates who had participated in the conference were torture victims as well.

Holding a photo of all the delegates who visited the village and the Israeli prison camps in South Lebanon, Maria said: This man spend seven years of torture at a prison in Bahrain, he is an archaeologist. This one, who is the representative of Association of Human Rights of Morocco, was also a former detainee. All of us who were at the committee we were once prisoners."

In a humble public ceremony at the main square of the village, which was attended by the citizens and public personalities of Kfar-Hamam, Maria folded the page that contained her prepared speech, looked at the people who had gathered in the small yard, and spoke from her heart.

"I had written a few words on this piece of paper for my speech here today, but the reality of this place makes me feel awkward," she said while standing on a makeshift podium on the back of a truck that was covered with carpets. "I was not fully informed and I was not prepared for what I would face in a village that I didn't even know its name. For five years as president of the International Rehabilitation Council for Torture Victims I traveled around the world and examined many torture victims, but I never came across a situation where an entire village of torture victims would be a beacon of freedom, democracy and at the forefront in the fight against torture."

In the winter of 2004—the period when this book was written—the situation in Lebanon may had improved from the years of the civil war, but many issues from the past still remained unsolved, like ghosts that were awaiting for their salvation.

On Jan. 29, 2004 and after complex and arduous negotiations, Israel released some 30 Lebanese prisoners and 400 Palestinians. Some of them had been in prison for over a decade, from the years of the civil war. In return, the Islamic group Hezbollah, returned to Israel the bodies of three of its soldiers who were killed in an ambush on 2002, and released a kidnapped Israeli businessman.

The Lebanese prisoners returned home to a hero's welcome. Tens of thousands of flag-waiving people—including scores of Hezbollah supporters—lined the airport highway for several miles, showering them in rice and rose petals. In Beirut, the government greeted the returning men with a red carpet, a brass band and an honor guard.

It was a hero's welcome as if the men were returning victorious from a battlefield.

At the same time in Israel a crowed had gathered at the Ben Gurion Airport near Tel Aviv to attend a memorial service for the three fallen soldiers.

One day later, on Jan. 30, 2004, and during the second and last phase of the complex prisoner swap, Israel returned to Lebanon the remains of 59 militants who were traded in exchange for information on missing airman Ron Arad, whose plane was shot down over Lebanon in 1986.

The return of the killed Lebanese fighters, who had died fighting Israel in southern Lebanon before the Israeli forces withdrew in 2000, was a reminder that past and present are firmly connected in the history of the area.

The remains of the dead militant guerrillas were taken to the capital Beirut in a slow procession of trucks coffins—like ghosts from the past that were awaiting salvation. After joint prayers that were attended by thousands of mourners, the dead fighters were handed over to their respective groups for funerals.

"I congratulate you. You are on your way to paradise," Hezbollah leader, Sheik Hassan Nasrallah, was quoted by The Associated Press as saying while leading a special prayer during a burial ceremony for 11 members of the militant group in a southern Beirut suburb.

If the black-turbaned cleric was right, then where is hell? Perhaps it is not that far away as some may have wanted to.

The presence of a 2,000-strong U.N. peacekeeping force in the southern Lebanese border with Israel—known as UNIFIL, or U.N. Interim Force in Lebanon—is a clear indication of how volatile the situation is still in the area. On Jan. 30, 2004 the U.N. Security Council in a typical procedure voted to extend the mission of the peacekeeping force for another six months, while calling on both sides to stop violating the U.N.-drawn boundary known as the "Blue Line."

The war may have ended—at least in paper—but the guns have not silenced yet and the screams from the former prison camps still echo in the ears of the torturers, while the souls of the dead fighters are still awaiting their salvation.

Do you still think that hell is a faraway place?

ONE WORLD—
ONE WOUND

From Iraq to Zimbabwe and from Greece to Lebanon, torture exhibits a unique universality and durability as an issue that touches the grayer areas of the human soul.

Torture never met any borders, while its cruel methods have shown no signs of corrosion with the pass of time. On the contrary, one can say that the exact opposite has happened as acts of torture not only continue to be performed in dozens of countries[25], but also the methods and technique vary very little from country to country.

"The patients in our rehab center in Athens come from countries that surround us, and those are mostly in the Middle East and North Africa," Maria noted during a meeting with the journalist at her house in central Athens. "Among those countries in the Middle East, the ones from where we have the most victims are Iraq, Turkey—with Turkish citizens as well as Kurds—as well as Iran. But Iraq and Turkey have indeed been the source for most of our victims."

Although the majority of the torture victims treated at the rehab center is men, records show that in recent years there has been a noted increase in the number of women who are seeking treatment. Maria explained that this rise in the number of female victims is in part due to a new policy by the rehab center by which the doctors are required to ask from their male patients to also bring their wives for examination—especially in cases where during psychotherapy there are indications that their wife may had also been a victim of torture.

"The woman has no right to appear as a victim of torture because of the Muslim perceptions," said Maria while holding the latest reports from the rehab center. "We had reached a point where only 3 percent of the victims in our center were women.

---

[25]   According to Amnesty International, in 2004 torture and ill-treatment by state agents were made in over 104 countries. In more than 70 countries torture or ill-treatment by state officials was widespread, while in over 80 countries people reportedly died as a result.

After that of course we started to probe more our male victims and those who said that their wives had also been tortured we would ask them to also bring them to the center. From that point on the number of women who have sought treatment in our rehab center have been increasing steadily, reaching as high as 13 and even 20 percent. So, we are talking about a lot of women."

According to Maria, some of the customary torture methods used against the male victims who have been treated at the center were unsystematic beatings[26], various forms of body suspension[27], electroshock[28], phalanx[29] (the beating on the soles of the feet), and cigarette burns on various parts of the body—a method which has become particularly common.

Unfortunately torture and violations of basic human rights, are not only found in countries that are in the greater neighborhood of Greece, but also in dozens more countries and in all continents across the globe.

Central and Latin America—Colombia

Although the majority of the countries in Latin America are viewed as democracies with democratically elected governments and with constitutions that provide guarantees for the protection of human rights, several countries are faced with instability even today.

The area of Latin America is "rich" in torture victims that have been left behind by vicious dictatorships, as well as by state security agents who until today practice torture methods in their day-to-day work. As a result, the psychological consequences of such cruel and inhumane practices continue to exist today, perpetuated by the fact that very few of the torturers have ever been arrested or even convicted of their crimes.

---

[26] Unsystematic beating includes is carried out with kicking and punching, but also whipping with wooden sticks, metallic pipes, electric cables and rifle butts.

[27] The various forms of body suspension included the hanging from the hands like a cross, and the Palestinian hanging where both hands and feet are tied in the back and passed through a wooden log. This last method causes permanent damage to the joints of the shoulders, which medically they are identified as the "Cold Shoulder Syndrome."

[28] The electroshock was very widespread in Iraq. In some cases it was used in the form of the "Apollo Chair," a metallic chair that was also known as the "Apollo Machine." The machine—devised by SAVAK, the Shah's secret police in Iran—it delivered an electric shock to sensitive parts of the body, while a steel helmet covered the prisoner's head to amplify their screams.

[29] Phalanx is the beating on the soles of the feet. In Iraq in most cases they would place the prisoner's inside a tire of a car until he could no longer move his legs and then they would hit him on the soles of his feet.

In Colombia, a country where a decade-old civil war—known as "La Violencia"—between conservatives and liberals left thousands of Colombians dead until 1958, violence has become a central feature in the social fabric of the country.

Today, the main actors in the violence are the guerrillas of the Revolutionary Armed Forces of Colombia—known by its acronym as FARC[30]—and the right-wing paramilitary groups organized by drug-traffickers, such as the United Self-Defense Forces of Colombia, also known by its acronym as AUC[31]. Of course the victim from this armed conflict is none else than the ordinary citizens of Colombia, who like in the civil war have learned to live with fear and pay the heaviest price of all.

"Civilians continued to be the principal victims of political violence," Amnesty International said in its 2004 report for Colombia. "The human rights situation in Colombia remained critical, its civilians[32] targeted by all sides in the conflict: the security forces, army-backed paramilitaries and armed opposition groups. Despite an agreed ceasefire and demobilization of some combatants, paramilitary forces were again responsible for widespread abuses. Security policies introduced by the government drew civilians further into the conflict."

The international human rights watchdog notes in its report that further evidence of spill-over from Colombia's internal war was seen in neighboring countries. Specifically it pointed out to the frequent border skirmishes that were reported in Venezuela and Ecuador, where the number of Colombians seeking shelter grew.

For 40 years now Colombians live under renewed states of emergency, a time period in which Colombia will have the highest murder rate[33] than any other country

---

[30]   The FARC, a guerrilla group which has its origins in the small Communist peasant groups that were formed in the 1920s and 1930s, was formed in 1964 and it is believed that it has as many as 18,000 fighters.

[31]   The AUC was formed in 1997 by drug-traffickers and landowners to combat rebel kidnappings and extortion. It is believed that it has maintained a 10,000-strong paramilitary force, while human rights groups have alleged that the army maintains ties with the group.

[32]   According to Amnesty International, in 2003 more than 3,000 civilians were killed for political motivates and at least 600 "disappeared." At the same time some 2,200 people were kidnapped, more than half by armed opposition groups and army-backed paramilitaries.

[33]   According to official state records by the Department of Planning, between 1987 and 1992 there were 77 homicides per 100,000 inhabitants, by far the highest murder rate in the world. In 1994 a report by the non-governmental group "Justice and Peace" noted that in the period between January and September there had been 1,268 murders for political reasons. During the same period there had also been some 1,378 kidnappings, reflecting a rise by 35 percent from the previous year.

on the planet. The country is also plagued by a spate of kidnappings[34] that have been carried out by both rebels and government forces. In 1997, Amnesty International filed a report in which it accused government and paramilitary groups for the deaths of hundreds of people. That year the international human rights group reported that most of the victims had been tortured before their death. It was that same year that dozens of people working for human rights organizations in Colombia were threatened and attacked, with 10 of them losing their life.

"The first time I feared for my life was in Bogotá. Never before in my life was I afraid, not even when I was in Manila during the military coup," said Maria during an interview at her house in Athens while flipping through photos from her recent trip to Colombia. She visited Bogotá in 2003 for a conference on torture organized by a regional anti-torture network.

Maria explained that they had decided to organize the conference in Bogotá in an effort to strengthen the local anti-torture center, which is a member of the Latin American and Caribbean Network of Health Professional Institutions Against Torture, Impunity, and Other Human Rights Violations[35].

"Our center in Bogotá is one of the best in terms of organization and it is cooperating with other non-governmental groups that operate in the country under very heroic conditions," Maria said. "I want to note that most of the people who are working at our center have personally received threats for their life and that they have been conducting their daily lives under specific guidelines by the High Commissioner of the United Nations."

In March 1997 the U.N. Human Rights Committee issued a series of observations and recommendations which deplored the fact that "gross and massive" human rights violations continued to be committed in Colombia by members of the armed forces, the police, paramilitary and guerrilla groups.

But all those mounting negative reports by international organizations and human rights groups will not manage to halt the country's downward path. The first powerful evidence of the international community's inability will come in 2000, a year when homicides and kidnappings will rise to record levels[36].

---

[34]   According to reports, kidnappings are not only carried out FARC rebels who kidnap citizens and tourists for ransom, but also by state security agents who are believed to be responsible for over 2,000 kidnappings and disappearances over a period of 15 years until 1994.

[35]   The Latin American and Caribbean Network of Health Professional Institutions Against Torture, Impunity, and Other Human Rights Violations are part of the global network of the International Rehabilitation Council for Torture Victims. Established in 1999, today it includes 16 rehab centers in 13 countries. The rehab center in Bogotá joined the network in 2000 along with the rehab centers of Brazil and Mexico.

[36]   According to Amnesty International, more than 4,000 people were victims of political killings in 2000, including two human rights defenders. At the same time, the human rights

And the future does not appear all that brighter.

A three-year truce that had been achieved by the former president Andres Pastrana with the rebels of FARC under which he had granted them some 42,000 sq. kilometers of land collapsed a few months prior to the 2002 elections, when Alvaro Uribe was elected president by winning the popular vote with the promise of crashing the Marxist guerrillas of FARC[37]. By the time of his election as president of Colombia, Uribe himself had survived 15 attempts on his life—with the most recent one a month prior to the elections—while his father had been gunned down some 20 year ago by Marxist rebels during a kidnap attempt.

In other countries of Latin America where democratic systems have been restored, such as Argentina, Brazil, Chile and Mexico, the widening gap between rich and poor has turned large populations in victims. According to the International Council for Torture Victims, in Mexico alone there are an estimated 20,000 victims of torture, mainly comprised of Zapotec Indians, community leaders in rural district and peasants.

"Political polarization and instability continued to affect Venezuela for much of the year," wrote Amnesty International in its report for 2004. "Levels of violence and protests diminished briefly after a referendum failed to unseat President Hugo Chavez, but the death of a high-profile special prosecutor in a car bombing raised fears of renewed political violence."

The situation in Haiti, which in the last few years has been characterized by a prolonged political instability, reached the levels of a crisis after a military uprising toppled the government of President Jean Bertrand Aristide. "Political violence and widespread human rights violations persisted, despite the presence of a U.N. military and police force," noted Amnesty International. "The severe loss of life and structural damage caused by a hurricane in September exacerbated instability and the breakdown of the rule of law, hampering distribution and international aid."

At the same time, public protests against violent crime, particularly kidnapping, spread throughout Latin America. "Vigilantism and mob lynching of suspected criminals were reported in countries including Guatemala, Mexico and Peru, where confidence in the security forces continued to evaporate," stressed the human rights group in its annual report.

But, aside from organized violence the countries of Latin and Central America have also been known for the impunity that has been enjoyed by the torturers and

---

watchdog reported that over 300 people "disappeared" while an estimated 300,000 people were internally displaced as a result of the continuing conflict. Also, at least 1,500 people were kidnapped in 2000 by armed opposition groups and paramilitary organizations. It is estimated that some 3,000 people are kidnapped in Colombia every year, with children accounting for 200 of such victims.

[37] Alvaro Uribe's plan included the doubling of professional soldiers and creating a militia of a million citizens.

military chiefs whose forces are responsible for appalling human rights violations. This long-lasting trend of impunity, though, appeared to change in 2004 after a series of court rulings came to show that those military strongmen and their torturers are not above the law.

In one such court decision, the Chilean Supreme Court lifted former President Augusto Pinochet's immunity from prosecution, allowing proceedings to be opened against him for human rights violations during "Operation Condor.[38]" At the same time an Argentine court issued an international warrant for the arrest of former Paraguayan President Alfredo Stroessner for his alleged involvement in human rights violations committed under "Operation Condor."

But even those efforts were not always met with success.

"Trial before civilian courts was no guarantee of justice, however," Amnesty International stressed in its annual report. "In Colombia, against all the evidence, charges were withdrawn against former General Rito Alejo del Rio, indicted for forming illegal paramilitary groups responsible for human rights violations in the 1990s."

Africa

Another area of the world where widespread human rights violations have raised serious concerns in the international community because of their barbaric nature is Africa.

"There torture has reached terrifying levels. Nowhere else have I seen so many amputations as I did when I was there," said Maria who has visited the African continent on several occasions in recent years. "One of the worst crimes has been the kidnapping of children, who are taken at training camps where they are taught some horrifying practices and are transformed into 12-year-old soldiers who in their effort to survive they kill and destroy everything in their path. Sierra Leone, Liberia, Congo and Sudan are only some examples of this practice, where you don't just see dead people in the streets, but butchered people. Most of the disfigured bodies that I have examined all these years as a doctor at our rehab center in Athens have come from Africa."

In 2004 the killings, abductions and rape by government forces and armed opposition groups remained widespread in armed conflicts in the Democratic Republic of Congo, Somalia, Sudan and Uganda. Meanwhile, the progress made

---

[38]   Operation Condor was a campaign of assassination and counter-terrorism that was jointly conducted between 1950 and 1980 by the intelligence and security services of the right-wing military dictatorships of Argentina, Bolivia, Brazil, Chile, Paraguay and Uruguay. According to the "terror archives" discovered in 1992 in Paraguay, some 50,000 people were murdered, another 30,000 "disappeared" and 400,000 imprisoned.

on a number of peace agreements remained fragile in Burundi, Cote d'Ivoire and Somalia, where sporadic outbreaks of violence persisted.

"Armed conflicts continued to bring widespread destruction to several parts of Africa in 2004, many of them fuelled by human rights violations. Refugees and internally displaced people faced appalling conditions," noted Amnesty International.

During that year Sudan was perhaps the land of the worst martyrdom on the African continent, with thousands of people being killed or raped in the escalating conflict in Darfur—western Sudan—and hundreds of thousands driven from their homes, many of them by government supported militias.

"Last September in a makeshift camp outside El Jeniena in Darfur, Sudan, I listened to a woman describe the attack on her village by government-supported militia," noted Irene Khan, the secretary general of Amnesty International, during a presentation of the group's annual report in London on May 2005. "So many men were killed that there were none left to bury the dead, and women had to carry out that sad task. I listened to young girls who had been raped by the militia and then abandoned by their own communities. I listened to men who had lost everything except their sense of dignity. These were ordinary, rural people. They may not have understood the niceties of 'human rights,' but they knew the meaning of 'justice.' They could not comprehend why the world was not moved to action by their plight."

In February of 2005 the United Nations said that some 70,000 people had died during the two-year conflict in Sudan's western Darfur region, but according to international human rights groups even that figure is off the mark because it is based on a study that covers only a period of six months. At the same time the U.N. estimated that some 2 million people of an estimated six million population have fled their homes to escape the conflict.

The secretary general of Amnesty International was very clear on who was responsible for the abiding violence: "In Darfur, the Sudanese government created a disaster for human rights and the international community did very little and too late to handle the crisis, betraying hundreds of thousands of people."

As she noted, Darfur was just another example of the deadly combination of apathy, pervasiveness and impunity that characterizes the landscape of human rights today. "Human rights are not just a promise that was not fulfilled, it is a promise that was betrayed," she remarked.

At the same time the situation in the eastern Democratic Republic of Congo remained volatile, with armed political groups continuing to carry out killings, rapes and other torture of civilians, and occasionally resumed fighting with rival forces.

Women and children continued to be the main victims in conflict areas. According to Amnesty International, women continued to be raped and subjected to other forms of sexual violence despite the ending of armed conflicts in the Central African Republic, Cote d'Ivoire and Liberia.

"In Darfur and eastern Democratic Republic of Congo, such abuse was used as a weapon of war against women and girls who had already experienced years of violence," the human rights watchdog stressed in its report.

The situation was so grim in Darfur that between October 2004 and February 2005 medical teams from the organization Doctors Without Borders treated more than 500 women and young girls who had been raped by government forces and militias that are supported by the government. The group noted then that this figure represents only a small fraction from the total number of victims, given the chronic under-reporting of rape. It added that almost a third of the women and girls who were victims of these attacks were raped by multiple perpetrators.

One of those victims was a 35-year-old Fur woman and mother of five children from Krolli village in South Darfur, who rushed with others to a police station for protection when government-backed Janjaweed militias attacked her village. But, according to Human Rights Watch, the police offered them no protection. As a result, civilians were held there for several days while the militia selected young women for rape and men were shot and tortured if they protested.

"They took girls away for long hours and brought them back later. Girls were crying, we knew they raped them," the woman told a team from the Human Rights Watch. "Some of us were raped in front of the crowd . . . I was sitting with the others on the bare floor, very exhausted, thirsty and scared. Two of them came to me, I resisted them and told them I did not want them but they did not like that. They hit me and decided to rape me in front of the others, one of them came from the back and started raping me . . . I could not move after that. Some young men tried to protect us from [rape], they received shots in both their legs. That was very painful and made them bleed, they could not move anymore. Others were hanged on the tree naked . . . It was just killing us to be raped and to see our men tortured like that."

According to Human Rights Watch, in some attacks documented by the group girls as young as seven and eight years old were raped, while some women were raped and then genitally mutilated.

The situation in parts of Africa was so brutish that women were not safe even at refugee camps, while many girls living below the poverty line remained at risk of being enrolled as child soldiers, beaten, forced into sexual slavery, and even killed. According to reports by human rights groups for 2004, in the Democratic Republic of Congo there was continued recruitment of child soldiers despite a planned demobilization of the army that was still largely to be implemented by the end of the year.

In Nigeria, according to the 2004 report by the Human Rights Watch, cases of extra-judicial killings, torture and ill-treatment of detainees and suspects remained the hallmarks of the Nigerian police. Some of the most common torture methods included unsystematic beatings with various objects, such as metallic pipes and whips, various forms of suspension from the ceiling and electroshock in the genitalia. The rights group notes that torture and other human rights violations were also widespread during 2004 in Uganda. An informal survey at Kigo Prison near Kampala, where "political" detainees are held, indicated in June 2003 that 90 percent of detainees/prisoners had been tortured during their prior detention by state military and security agencies. According to Human Rights Watch, some of the forms of torture used in Uganda included severe and repeated beatings with metal of wooden poles, cables, hammers and sticks with nails protruding; electroshock; male and female genital and body mutilation; and strangulation.

But 2004 was also a year that saw many positive developments for the African continent, such as the end of armed conflict in places like Burundi, Liberia and Angola, which in turn cleared the way for the return of thousands of refugees.

The year of 2004 also saw important developments on the issue of impunity for human rights violations in armed conflicts. The governments of the Democratic Republic of Congo and Uganda referred war crimes and crimes against humanity, war crimes and other serious violations to the International Criminal Court. Trials also started before the Special Court for Sierra Leone of people indicted for crimes against humanity, war crimes and other serious violations of international law, including rape, other forms of sexual violence and sexual slavery. According to Amnesty International, the Court had previously ruled that the general amnesty granted in the 1999 Lome peace agreement was "ineffective" in preventing it from prosecuting crimes against humanity and war crimes, and that Charles Taylor, the former President of Liberia, had no immunity from prosecution.

"Charles Taylor, indicted for 'bearing the greatest responsibility' for killings, mutilations, rape and other abuses through active support of armed opposition forces in Sierra Leone, remained in Nigeria," noted Amnesty International. "He had been granted refugee status, with apparent guarantees that he would be neither surrendered to the Special Court nor brought before Nigeria's own courts."

For Africa, a land of martyrdom for millions of people, the only path for salvation appears to be that of forgiveness and reconciliation.

"When we look around us at some of the conflict areas of the world, it becomes increasingly clear that there is not much of a future without forgiveness, without reconciliation," wrote Archbishop Desmond Tutu in his forward for the final report of the Truth and Reconciliation Commission of South Africa, which he chaired until 1997. "God has blessed us richly so that we might be a blessing to others. Quite improbably, we as South Africans have become a beacon of hope to others locked in deadly conflict that peace, that a just resolution, is possible. If it could happen in South Africa, then it can certainly happen anywhere else."

The Commission[39] investigated past human rights violations and the possible involvement of doctors in cases of torture and ill-treatment. According to the

---

[39]   The Truth and Reconciliation Commission of South Africa had three sub-committees—the
        Amnesty Committee, the Human Rights Violations Committee, and the Reparation and

Commission's final report, some 20,000 people declared to have suffered gross human rights violations in the period between 1960 and the first democratic elections of South Africa.

The work of the Commission will play a critical role in helping South Africa to turn page in one of the darkest chapters if its history, as the lure of amnesty will bring to surface answers to crimes that no prosecutor would be able to bring to court for decades—if ever.

Unfortunately the wise words of Archbishop Desmond Tutu will fall to deaf ears, especially in Africa where gross atrocities continue even today.

Balkans—Bosnia

But not even the Old Continent can claim a clean human rights record as the unceasing armed conflicts in the Balkans in the 1990s left behind tens of thousands of dead people, hundreds of thousands of refugees and an undetermined number of torture victims.

All sides without exception used torture. Villages were pillaged and left in ruins, women were abused and raped, and entire families were exterminated in the altar of religious fanaticism.

The three-year conflict in Bosnia alone, which started in 1992, left behind some 250,000 dead and missing people while half the population became refugees in neighboring countries. Although the reports of international organizations that investigated and recorded the brutishness of force used by all sides are numerous, one can get a fair idea of the atrocities by studying the findings of just one of them.

One of the many human rights reports compiled by independent bodies was that of the "Committee for the Collection of Data on Crimes Committed against Humanity and International Law." The six-member medical team investigated case of Serb victims of torture in Croat-Muslim detention camps. The Committee started its work in 1994 and concluded it in 1995, examining a total of 92 detainees in seven hospitals in Bosnia. Their detention time varied from 31 days to one year.

According to the report of the Committee, 45 percent of the respondents examined had—as a result of their torture—developed a post-traumatic stress disorder (PTSD), while all but four of them exhibited scars, deformities, and disfigurement on their skin, and they missed several teeth. In total, their torturers used 38 different forms of physical torture, 11 methods of psychological torture, and 14 methods that combined physical and mental torture.

Some of the torture methods were so gruesome that were indicative of how perverted was the mind of the torturers. Those included: firing of blank cartridges

---

Rehabilitation Committee—which were responsible for investigate and offer amnesty for violations and crimes committed during the era of apartheid.

into the anus of the victim (death occurs five to six hours later with grave pain as a result of internal hemorrhage); putting out cigarettes by pressing them in the victim's mouth; tying the victim's genitals to his ears with an electric wire and turning on electricity; nailing the victim's two hands to a board with a hammer and forcing the victim to walk around like that for a whole day; cutting parts of the victim's body, like the eyes or genitals and forcing them to swallow them; forcible pushing of objects into the victim's anus, mouth, eyes, nose or ears; forcing victims to eat the meat of a roasted newborn; individual or group rape of female detainees, including anal rape and fellatio; forced placement of captured female adolescents in brothels and making them work as prostitutes until they conceived and were in their seventh or eighth month of their pregnancy; forcing inmates, especially brothers or a father and his son to engage in mutual fellatio or to have anal intercourse; and defecating or urinating in the victim's mouth.

Those who managed to get out of those hellish places alive had very little psychological strength, and would end up in mental clinics. According to the Committee, some 1 million people from the former Yugoslavia were in need of psychosocial and mental health assistance in 1995—the year they compiled the report. The Committee noted in its findings that the torturers did not only aim at the physical and mental destruction of the detainees but also wanted to create a climate of terror and fear which spreads like a virus from the victims to their relatives and then to entire communities.

Of course the wars in the Balkans have ceased and the guns have silenced, but who can say with certainty how long it would take those societies to return to a healthy state. Until that day comes, hatred will be simmering inside those communities and will be desperately seeking a chance to show its ugly face.

HELPING HAND

The view of the world from a satellite can be very impressive, with various shades of color depicting the oceans and embossed shapes that illustrate the mountains and valleys, but the picture from the ground—at least with regard the human rights—is rather dark.

What appears to be a paradise as you see it from afar, when you come closer you realize that in reality it is merely a mirage. At least this is the view held by thousands of people who every year fall victims of torture and ill-treatment in their countries by ruthless leaders and authoritarian regimes.

Fortunately this picture is not entirely dark, but it has different shades of gray and even white—strokes of brash that at times are made by a small brash and others by a larger one. The "artist" who makes these "artistic modifications" on this global canvas of human rights is no other than the international network of non-governmental rights groups and humanitarian organizations, who work restlessly in every corner of the planet as a watchful guardian of human values, which are under constant siege.

It is a helping hand that all these years is extended unselfishly to the victims, while facing itself enormous difficulties in its work from authoritarian regimes as well as because of the risks taken by the human rights workers in conflict zones.

Amnesty International

One of the pioneer non-governmental human rights organizations in Amnesty International, whose action the past 40 years has covered the five continents of this planet with over 1.8 million members, supporters and subscribers in over 150 countries.

"Although they come from many different backgrounds and have widely different political and religious beliefs, they are united by a determination to work for a world where everyone enjoys human rights," said Amnesty International in a statement about its members worldwide.

The group's mission, as defined by itself, is to undertake research and action focused on preventing and ending grave abuses of the rights to physical and mental integrity, freedom of conscience and expression, and freedom from discrimination, within the context of its work to promote all human rights.

56

Some of global campaigns by Amnesty International that continued in 2004 were those against torture, the death penalty, child soldiers, as well as the protection of refugee rights.

"When you are afraid that someone is at risk of torture, you need to do two things: You need to act fast, and you need to shout loud," Amnesty International notes in a message for its campaign "Stop Torture." "Amnesty International hears that a man, woman or child has been picked up by police and may be at risk of torture. Within hours they can mobilize a network of 75,000 people in over 70 countries to send urgent faxes, letters and e-mails to the authorities responsible, all saying the same things: stop torture, respect human rights."

Amnesty International says the scale of pressure is such that few governments[40] can ignore.

"The torturer aims to isolate you, to cut all your links with the outside world. But Amnesty International was able to break that isolation . . . When I saw my wife, I knew that my case had become public. I knew they could no longer kill me," said Professor Luiz Rossi, in a statement released through Amnesty International. He was the subject of Amnesty's first "Urgent Action" in April 1973.

Among the thousands of people that Amnesty International has helped is Maria, who after her release from the prison-island of Gyaros she became a member of the group's executive board in Greece. Maria will become a member of Amnesty International's Greek office in 1980, joining one of its teams that were responsible for writing protest letters and for organizing various campaigns in the country. Three years later, in 1983, she will be given the task to coordinate the work of Amnesty's newly-established medical team at the Aglaia Kyriakou Hospital. The volunteer team, which comprised 16 doctors and one psychologist, would offer for years its valuable assistance to refugees and torture victims from numerous countries.

Another global campaign by Amnesty International is that against the death penalty, which the human rights group characterizes as the "ultimate cruel, inhuman and degrading punishment." The organization notes that this form of punishment is irrevocable and can be inflicted on the innocent, while it also stresses that it has never been shown to deter crime more effectively than other punishments. In spite this, according to Amnesty International, some 83 countries[41] retain and use the death penalty today.

"These figures include only cases known to Amnesty International; the true figures were certainly higher. The vast majority of executions worldwide are carried out in

---

[40]   Amnesty International says that 1 in 3 of the 500 letters that it sends every year have some positive impact.

[41]   According to Amnesty International, in 2002 at least 1,562 people were executed in 31 countries, while at least 3,248 people were sentenced to death in 67 countries.

a tiny handful of countries. In 2002[42], 81 percent of all known executions took place in China, Iran and the U.S.," the rights group said in a statement for its campaign against the death penalty.

The campaign by Amnesty International envisions a global abolishment of the death penalty, especially in countries where the death penalty is used against child offenders, in spite the fact that executions of people under 18 years of age is prohibited by international law. But there are some signs of hope. According to Amnesty International, in November 2003 some 76 countries and territories had abolished the death penalty for all crimes, while another 16 countries had abolished it for all but exceptional crimes such as wartime crimes.

The work of Amnesty International, though, does not end there. The human rights group faces the challenge of another modern violation of basic human rights: the recruitment of child soldiers[43] and their use in conflict zones, particularly in Africa. This development could not leave indifferent an international rights group like Amnesty International since it knew well that without any pressure on those governments the victims of this inhumane practice would become the proxy of an entire generation that would be ailing both physically and mentally.

"I would like to give you a message. Please do your best to tell the world what is happening to us, the children. So that other children don't have to pass through this violence," said a 15-year-old girl who escaped from the Lord's Resistance Army in Uganda, in a statement released through Amnesty International.

This is also the goal of Amnesty's campaign, which has also found the warm support of the United Nations. The work by Amnesty International is deemed one of the most influential on a global scale, and it is recognized both by the victims that it has helped as well as by international organizations that are active in the area of human rights.

". . . if there's lots of pressure—like from Amnesty International or some foreign countries—we might pass them on to a judge. But if there's no pressure, then they're dead," said a former torturer from El Salvador in a statement released by Amnesty International.

Jean-Pierre Hocke, the former United Nations High Commissioner for Refugees said once: It's a worn cliché, but if Amnesty did not exist, it would have to be invented. It is simply unique."

---

[42]   Amnesty International reports that in 2002 at least 1,060 people were executed in China, while over 113 executions were carried out in Iran. That same year some 71 people were executed in the U.S.

[43]   According to Amnesty International, more than half a million children under-18 have been recruited worldwide in government armed forces, paramilitaries, civil militia and a wide variety of non-state armed groups in more than 85 countries. At any one time, more than 300,000 of these children are actively fighting as soldiers with government armed forces and armed political groups.

International Rehabilitation Council for Torture Victims

Another international non-governmental human rights organization of equal importance is the International Rehabilitation Council for Torture Victims (IRCT), which is based in Copenhagen since 1985 and has over 200 rehab centers worldwide.

The IRCT is an independent, international health professional organization that promotes and supports the rehabilitation of torture victims and works for the prevention of torture worldwide. The organization has special consultative status with the U.N. Economic and Social Council and the U.N. Department of Public Information, and participatory status with the Council of Europe—the human rights watchdog of the European Union.

The IRCT notes that although freedom from torture is a universal and fundamental human right for all, as guaranteed under international law and defined in the U.N. Convention against Torture, the U.N. every year receives reports on acts of torture from more than 60 countries. But according to the IRCT this figure in reality is even higher, as according to other sources government-sanctioned torture is committed in more than 130 countries.

"Torture is the intentional infliction of severe pain or suffering for a specific purpose. Torture is used to obtain information or a confession, to punish, to take revenge, or to create terror and fear within a population. The aim of torture is not to kill the victim, but to break down the victim's personality," the IRCT explains.

The Council notes that methods of physical and psychological torture are remarkably similar worldwide, with most techniques seeking to prolong the victim's pain and fear as long as possible without leaving visible evidence on their bodies. According to the Council, some of the most common methods of physical torture include beating, electric shocks, stretching, submersion, suffocation, and burns. Also, some of the common methods of psychological torture include isolation, threats, humiliation, mock executions, and witnessing the torture of others. Rape and sexual assault are also a form of torture, and are commonly practiced against women during arrest or imprisonment, or during conflicts and civil war.

The consequences of torture reach far beyond the immediate physical pain, according the Council, as the effects can be physical, psychological, and social. "In addition to the physical effects of torture, victims of torture can suffer from flashbacks (or intrusive thoughts), severe anxiety, insomnia, nightmares, depression, memory lapses, and a breakdown in social relations. They often feel guilt and shame, triggered by the humiliation they have endured or by a sense that they have betrayed themselves or their friends and family. All such symptoms are normal human responses to abnormal and inhumane treatment," the IRCT says.

According to the Council, victims of torture can include politicians, union leaders, journalists, health professionals, human rights defenders, people in detention or prison, members of ethnic minorities, student leaders, and ordinary citizens—children as well as adults.

The IRCT with its vast global network of rehabilitation centers for torture victims offers medical as well as psychological and legal support to the victims and their families. The work of the Council and of its rehab centers is truly unique. At the same time this non-governmental organization is recognized internationally for its work in the research and recording of acts of torture worldwide, as it maintains the world's largest collection[44] of materials on torture, the rehabilitation of torture victims, and the prevention of torture.

At the same time the IRCT continues its work with intervention in conflict zones—during 1993-1997 the Council provided psychological help to Bosnian war victims in Croatia and Bosnia-Herzegovina—as well as by providing training and support to local health professionals who treat victims of torture.

The aim of rehabilitation, according to the Council, is to empower the torture victim to regain the capacity, confidence, and ability to resume as full a life as possible. The process is painstaking and long.

"Rebuilding the life of an individual whose inherent dignity has been destroyed takes time. One of the greatest challenges for health professionals and other caregivers is to gain the trust and confidence of their client, and being available for the client whenever needed," the Council notes.

Although the work of the Council and of its rehab centers is vital, dozens are the governments that not only don't support the work of the local rehab centers but are also their fiercest enemies. As the Council notes, the rehab centers aside from their medical and legal work, are also symbols of triumph over the terror of torture that those regimes have created in their citizenry. In 2000, the IRCT conducted urgent actions and mobilized international support in order to provide protection for health professionals and other caregivers at risk in Indonesia (Aceh), Turkey, and Zimbabwe.

"Torture is a political act, and so too is the rehabilitation of torture victims. Through awareness, reporting, media campaigns, local community development, documentation, training and education, centers can play a key role in the promotion of democracy, co-existence, and respect for human rights," the IRCT notes.

Although dozens[45] of countries have yet to ratify the U.N. Convention against Torture, the Council says that the steps that have been made so far are important and those achievements were realized after years of hard work.

"Nevertheless, the political will and legislative measures needed to eradicate torture are an important first step, and for this reason the IRCT actively lobbies governments to ratify and implement the U.N. Convention," the Council says.

---

[44]   The International Rehabilitation Council for Torture Victims has started to create the "Global Torture Victims Information System," which will be the only one of its kind in the world.

[45]   According to the International Rehabilitation Council for Torture Victims, as of February 2001, 123 U.N. Member States (of a total of 192) had ratified the U.N. Convention against Torture.

In 2003 the IRCT joined 20 other international rights organizations—including Amnesty International—in writing petitions and collecting signatures in order to put pressure upon world governments to stop torture by ratifying and implementing the U.N. Convention against Torture.

"I hope that the movement against torture will maintain this important work and will keep putting pressure on governments and other decision-makers to do what is in their power to eradicate torture," said Dalai Lama in a message to the IRCT on June 26, 2003—the international day against torture. "I am deeply grateful to all of the participants for their efforts in this respect and I encourage you to continue this meaningful work together."

A few months later, on Sept. 24, 2003, Dalai Lama will once again praise the work of the IRCT when he will travel to New York to attend a ceremony in which the Council will be awarded the Conrad N. Hilton Humanitarian Prize—the world's largest humanitarian award. Previous recipients of the award include the Doctors Without Borders.

During the ceremony Dalai Lama characterized the work of the IRCT as "a spiritual act of compassion . . . compassion in action," while he noted the importance of attending to individuals who have suffered at the hands of others.

On Aug. 22, 2003, when it was officially announced that the recipient of the award will be the IRCT, Steven Hilton, President of the Conrad N. Hilton Foundation said from Los Angeles: "By addressing the unimaginable suffering of men, women, and even children who have endured torture, IRCT personifies the purpose of the Hilton Humanitarian Prize, which is to recognize and support the work of organizations alleviating human suffering throughout the world."

Jens Modvig, then secretary general of the IRCT, had said: "May the (prize) bring hope to all of who have suffered as a result of torture. May it bring shame and condemnation upon the perpetrators. And, may it strengthen our resolve, and encourage others to join us, in our efforts for a world without torture."

Today, the non-governmental anti-torture organization has 10 regional networks worldwide with hundreds of medical rehab centers in areas like Asia, Latin and Central America, Africa, Europe and in the United States.

The Medical Rehabilitation Center for Torture Victims in Athens

One of the hundreds of rehab centers of IRCT is located in Athens, Greece. The Medical Rehabilitation Center for Torture Victims (MRCTV) has been operating[46] in Athens since 1989, providing essential services to hundreds of torture victims every year.

---

[46]   The Medical Rehabilitation Center for Torture Victims is operating with funds from the European Union and the Greek state.

Maria, because of the experience she had gained when she worked with victims of torture as a supervisor of Amnesty's medical teams in Greece, she was chosen to launch the anti-torture rehab center in Athens.

When the MRCTV was founded it broke new ground in Greece, a country where although the days of the junta were long-gone, the subject of torture was still a very sensitive topic. The first steps for the creation of the center were very careful as through this effort its founders wanted to present the political unity that existed on the issue of torture—a unity that in turn would provide a relative protection for the work of rehab center.

"Of course the year was 1989 but we still had the scars of the dictatorship and a political instability integrated inside us. Not that there was any instability but we—and particularly me—still felt like that," said Maria in one of the several interviews that the journalist conducted at her house in Athens. "So, facts like which party was in power and which political party would win the next elections created insecurity for the viability of our rehab center."

In an effort to ensure a political stability in relation with the viability of the rehab center, the first board of directors comprised people who represented the entire political spectrum so that the center would never be threatened by a change in the government. As a result, the position of the president was given to Fotis Kouvelis, an MP with the Left Coalition; Popi Nikolaou, a European MP with the Greek Socialist Party was named vice president; and the position of the secretary general was given to Nikita Kalkamanis, an MP with the conservative party of New Democracy.

The selection of the board members, aside from their political identity was also based on a distinctive sensitivity they had exhibited on the issue of torture, which went beyond party lines. Years later, when the rehab center had established a strong footing in Greek society, the synthesis of the board changed to include more scientists and experts such as doctors, psychiatrists, law professors and social workers.

Maria, as the medical director of the center, continued to play a central role in all examinations of suspected torture victims, while her opinion would carry a lot of weight in the decision on whether the center would issue a certificate of torture victim in each individual case.

"The first medical examination in our center was, and continues to be conducted by me," Maria noted.

But because of the nature of torture that the victims have suffered, some of them exhibit various diseases and health complaints that pertain to different medical specialties, and because the rehab center does not have enough money to support such a large medical staff, most of the victims—if not all of them—are examined by doctors who volunteer their services to the center.

"The money of the rehab center were never such that we could afford to have doctors to conduct all those examinations, so we created a network of volunteer doctors—most of them top names in the Greek medical community—who offered their services for free," Maria explained. "Also, members of the medical staff at various hospitals went out of their way to offer us critical help in the first years, even risking their jobs at times. During those years we were also unable to provide any medication to the victims. Slowly we have reached the point where we can provide some medicines by using some of the center's funds, which are getting fewer and fewer."

But, the economic viability[47] of the anti-torture center is at risk. The financial problem faced by the anti-torture center is absolutely disproportionate to the value of the rehabilitation work that is offered to the hundreds of torture victims every year, as well as of the necessity to continue its work in the coming years.

In 2003 alone, the rehab center issued some 93 certificates to an equivalent number of torture victims, while it also examined and provided medical, psychological and legal services to hundreds more victims. At the same time, it organized several national and international conferences, while it also held numerous training seminars on human rights for police officers.

The needs over the years have grown so much that a second rehab center had to open its doors in the northern port city of Thessaloniki—Greece's second largest city—while a network of anti-torture centers had to be created in the Balkans in 1993 in order to cover the rising population of torture victims that was created by the Balkan wars.

"In 1993, amidst the war in the Balkans, I thought that we should give an example of a different perception of things," said Maria in explaining how the idea was born for the creation of the Balkan network. "I thought that the doctors from the warring sides with their cooperation could set an example for others. So, I organized here the first Balkan conference with participants from mainly conflict areas of the time such as Sarajevo, Zagreb, and Belgrade, while the conference was also attended by health professionals from Albania and Bulgaria."

Maria described this first meeting of the Balkan network as "exciting," since the television crews were "filming the Bosnian and Croatian representatives sitting next to each other and having a conversation. In other words there was solidarity among the doctors of both sides who were faced with a common problem."

The network, known as the Balkan Network for the Prevention of Torture and Rehabilitation of Victims, also known by its acronym as BA.N., today has 11 medical rehab centers[48], while its activities are coordinated by the medical rehab center in Athens.

---

[47] At the beginning the European Union and the U.N. Volunteer Fund provided some 80 percent of the funds needed for the operation of the rehab center in Athens, and the rest was based on volunteer work. Today, the funds from the European Union are diminishing year-by-year, accounting for just 50 percent and forcing the rehab center to seek additional funds from domestic sources.

[48] The Balkan Network for the Prevention of Torture and Rehabilitation of Victims (www. bannet.org) has 11 medical rehab centers including those in Sofia, Tirana, Sarajevo, Belgrade, Zagreb, Pristine, Athens and Thessaloniki.

"Since 1993 this network had been working continuously and is deemed as one of the best peripheral networks of the IRCT," said Maria. "Besides, it was the first network that was organized within the framework of the Council."

After the end of the war Maria visited some of the most hard-hit areas. The scene was disheartening.

"I will never forget my visit to Sarajevo right after the war, where the graves had penetrated into the streets and the square of the city. All sidewalks were full of graves. I will never forget that scene. I will never forget," Maria said while recalling her visit there.

In 1991 and while the bombardment of Yugoslavia had just ceased, the Balkan network called its fourth conference in Athens in order to coordinate its work in the area, which was still counting its wounds as a new wave of refugees was looming over the horizon.

Maria again gave her own view about the events that were unfolding.

"A war just ended but a new war is starting," she said in her speech before an audience of health professionals from Yugoslavia, Albania, Croatia, Bosnia and Bulgaria. "It is a war marked by the return of those people who survived the bombing and who now will be faced with a new reality—that of killed relatives, destroyed homes, and lost countries. Those people, based on the experience that we have accumulated over the years, will exhibit symptoms of PTSD (Post-Traumatic Stress Disorder), which means nightmares, loss of trail of thought, loss of memory and in some cases even aggressive behavior."

Investigations and studies by several independent committees and human rights groups show that both sides used torture against one another during the war.

"I remind my fellow countrymen, the Serbs: you must face reality around you; and the fellow Albanians: it is very easy to cross the road between being a victim and a victimizer," noted Stefan Lilic, professor of international law from Belgrade.

Several years have passed since the end of the war in Yugoslavia and the Balkans still live with finger on the trigger, while thousands of refugees still wait for the day when they will return to their homes, their countries, and the graves of their relatives.

Perhaps finding the money needed to sustain the operations of the medical rehab center in Athens is hard, but if the anti-torture center closes its doors one day because the European Union and the Greek state could not spare a few change for humanitarian purposes then the reality for the thousands of torture victims will be much harder.

"When I inaugurated our rehab center I made a very negative but at the same time very positive wish. I wished that the center would close as soon as possible. Not because there are no funds to support its work for which it has been praised, but because there will be no more torture victims," Maria noted. "I still make this wish every year, but it has yet to become real. On the contrary, year-by-year the situation worsens. In the past we used to talk only about victims of torture, but now we also talk about victims of war."

The United Nations High Commissioner for Refugees

Another international organization that has made its own strokes of brush on the global canvas of human rights is the United Nations High Commissioner for Refugees (UNHCR), which for over 50 years[49] has been offering assistance to millions of refugees and asylum seekers worldwide. During its half century of humanitarian work, the agency provided assistance to at least 50 million people, earning two Nobel Peace Prizes[50].

When the agency was established it was given a limited three-year mandate to help resettle 1.2 million European refugees left homeless by World War II. But as time passed the agency's mission had to change, as it had to adjust to the ever-changing global map of small- and large-scale conflicts that generate fresh waves of refugees. As a result it expanded from a relatively small, specialized agency to an organization with offices in more than 120 countries, a $1 billion annual budget, and a capacity to provide both legal protection and material relief in major emergencies.

At the same time, and while the definition of a refugee remained the same— covering only people who had fled their homeland and sought sanctuary in a second country to escape persecution for their religion, race, nationality and political beliefs—there was a rising number of people in similar separate circumstances but who do not legally qualify as refuges and are therefore not eligible for normal relief and protection.

As a result, the refugee agency started to include in its programs populations that have come to be known to the world as Internally Displaced Persons or IDPs[51], people who had fled their homes—generally during a civil war—but have stayed in their home countries rather than seeking refuge abroad.

But the agency's work does not end there. The U.N. refugee agency also provides emergency relief—such as shelter, food, water, sanitation and medical care—in areas

---

[49]   The UNHCR was established in 1950. Today, the U.N. refugee agency is one of the world's principal humanitarian agencies, with a staff of more than 5,000 personnel helping some 20 million people in more than 120 countries.

[50]   The UNHCR was the recipient of the Nobel Peace Prize in 1954 and 1981.

[51]   According to the UNHCR, globally there are an estimated 20 to 25 million IDPs, while the refugee agency helps some 6.3 million of them.

that experienced, or still experience, armed conflict, such as Afghanistan[52], Timor, Africa[53], the Balkans[54], Asia[55], and the Middle East[56].

The U.N. refugee agency notes that every country in the world has been affected by a refugee crisis, either by being directly involved in a conflict or by providing shelter and aid to the displaced.

"In many cases, today's neighbor is tomorrow's refugee," says the UNHCR. "They have lost their homes, jobs, community and often family. They are not a threat, but they do need temporary help until they can reestablish their lives."

In 2000 the UNHCR needed over $100 million to cover the needs of the millions of refugees who were still leaving in neighboring countries due to remaining tensions. More than half of the money went to the Federal Republic of Yugoslavia, which at the time had more than 700,00 refugees on its soil—the largest refugee population in Europe at the time. In addition, according to UNHCR records, up until January 2002 there were about 389,000 refugees in Serbia and Montenegro while the number of internally displaced persons was about 230,000. During the same period, in Kosovo the U.N. refugee agency had recorded over 20,000 refugees from the Former Yugoslav Republic of Macedonia, while there were another 10,000 people who were internally displaced in Kosovo.

Until 2004 a large number of those refugees were still living in refugee camps and the dream of one day returning to their homes, their countries, was starting to fade.

---

[52] In Afghanistan, in spite the return of some 4.6 million refugees, in 2004 there were still some 4 million Afghans who were living in foreign countries while another 750,000 were internally displaced. In 2002 the Afghans comprised the largest refugee population that the U.N. agency provided assistance.

[53] In West Africa, the first five months of 2001 some 60,000 refugees were relocated to safer camps inside Guinea following fresh clashes broke out at the borders with Sierra Leone and Liberia. In Central Africa, Tanzania during 2001 had the largest refugee population in Africa, mainly hosting refugees from Burundi, who at the start of 2001 were also the second largest refugee group in the world cared by the UNHCR. In Angola, two million people had been uprooted in 2001 because of internal conflict. In the Horn of Africa, in May 2001—nearly one year after an intermittent war between Ethiopia and Eritrea ended—the UNHCR was able to start a major repatriation operation for the return of 174,000 long-time Eritrean refugees from neighboring Sudan.

[54] In the Balkans, an estimated 1.8 million civilians have returned to their home countries in the last few years, but another 1.3 million persons remained displaced and throughout the first months of 2001.

[55] In Sri Lanka the UNHCR in 2001 was assisting more than 700,000 people internally displaced by the ongoing civil conflict.

[56] In the Middle East, around 3.8 million people are registered with the U.N. Relief and Works Agency—the organization responsible for Palestinian refugees.

"People can go to the moon easily these days," Tihomir Stanimorovic, a Serb refugee from Kosovo, told the UNHCR. "But, in the Balkans we can't even go the few miles back to our homes."

The UNHCR in 2004 signed a protocol of cooperation with the Medical Rehabilitation Center for Torture Victims in Athens, Greece—one of the very few that it has signed worldwide—as ever since it opened its doors the U.N. refugee agency has been a steady "supplier" of refugees who had been victims of torture in their home countries.

"The Medical Rehabilitation Center for Torture Victims is a trusted partner of the UNHCR in Greece," said Robert White, the UNHCR representative in the country at the time, in an interview for the book. "The treatment is one issue and recognizing someone as a refugee is another. Both of them, though, are fundamental for the future of those people. The assistance to the victims of torture should be a priority for all of us, whether we are members of a humanitarian organization or members of a government."

Cooperation like this one have assisted the Greek state in formulating new immigration laws and regulations regarding the asylum process, while at the same time function as a safety net by providing invaluable services to thousands of refugees and asylum-seekers.

The humanitarian work of these two groups has certainly made the Greek canvas of human rights to be less black and a bit grayer—even a bit whiter in some cases.

September 11th

The fear of international rights groups that the time was nearing when human rights would no longer top the global agenda due to a greater reorganization in the global political stage will come true much sooner than anyone feared.

The Sept. 11, 2001 will become a turning point, not just for America, which by dusk will be mourning over 3,000 dead civilians—but for the entire humanity, as the events that would follow the dramatic terrorist attacks will serve as a time machine that would take world many years back in terms of the human rights.

It was 8:45 a.m. in New York when the American Airlines jetliner with Flight No. 11 was crashing on one of the Twin Towers at a speed of 760 kilometers per hour (472 miles per hour). Eighteen minutes later, on 9:03 a.m., a second aircraft of United Airlines with Flight No. 175 would also crash with great ferocity—at a speed exceeding the 950 kilometers per hour (590 miles per hour)—on the second skyscraper. Forty minutes later, a third jetliner would slam into the Pentagon in Washington DC. America was awakening violently that morning and as the hours were passing an entire nation was wondering: if Washington DC and New York aren't safe then where is it safe to live?

The terrorists had achieved their goal. Terror and fear had made everyone's blood to turn cold, not just in America where people were watching their own people to be jumping from the windows of the skyscraper to escape the flames, but also the millions of people around the globe who were watching live the horrifying scenes on their televisions.

Everyone knew that nothing would ever be the same because such an unprecedented attack meant that an unprecedented response—whatever that may entail.

Indeed, two days after the terrorist attacks in New York and Washington DC, U.S. President George Bush announced that the Saudi billionaire Osama bin Laden was the mastermind behind the attacks, while the next day called up 50,000 reservists. A month later, on October 7, America and Great Britain were launching a joint military assault in Afghanistan. According to independent sources, over 3,500 ordinary Afghans would lose their life from U.S. and British fire until March 2002.

When a Pentagon official was asked by reporters to comment on the death of 93 civilians who were killed by airstrikes carried out by U.S. warplanes on Oct. 22

and Oct. 23, 2001 in a village about 40 kilometers (25 miles) north of Kandahar, he remarked: "The people there are dead because we wanted them dead," explaining that according to their information the victims were Taliban sympathizers.

It was now obvious that what until that day we were considering as vested rights of a society of humans were now being contested. The time machine was warming up.

"After having reached a point where we were discussing 3rd Generation Rights, such as the right for a clean environment and a series of other rights, we made a U-turn and started to contest the 1st Generation Rights, which include the right to life, with a war against the al Qaeda and the Taliban without any considerations for the civilian populations who would be the victims of this assault," said Maria during a discussion about human rights at her house in Athens.

The rapidly deteriorating human rights situation came immediately to the attention of rights groups, including the International Rehabilitation Council for Torture Victims. Recognizing the graveness of the situation and the negative consequences it would have for human rights, the IRCT in its annual conference, held on the Greek island of Syros on Nov. 21, 2001, issued a declaration that soon became known as "The Syros Declaration on Torture, Terrorism, and War."

In the Declaration, among other things, the IRCT expressed its deep concern about the devastating loses to individuals, their families, and communities resulting from the 9/11 terrorist attacks on the United States and the subsequent attacks on Afghanistan. The Council also expressed serious concern over the proposed and actual use of torture to extract information from detainees and alleged terrorists.

The IRCT also sent letters to three international organizations, the UN Committee against Torture; the UN Human Rights Committee; and the European Committee for the Prevention of Torture, in which it expressed the same concerns that were addressed in the Syros Declaration.

But the Syros Declaration and the letters will fall to deaf ears inside the international community, which had turn into a spectator to the dramatic events that were unfolding—both politically and militarily.

It will soon become clear that the war in Afghanistan was only the beginning. Within a few months after the 9/11 attacks, U.S. state and federal law enforcement agencies will start arresting hundreds of Muslims living across America, and detaining them for months without ever filing any charges against them or notifying their families. In total isolation from the outside world and with the right for legal representation being quashed for most of them, more than 700 people remained in detention until January 2004 without knowing why. All of a sudden, in America—a country which has prospered mainly because of its ability to attract foreign scientists and skilled workers from abroad for decades, and which has been a champion of tolerance and equal rights for all irrespective of their color, race and ethnicity—being a Muslim was a crime and you had to be arrested.

During the same period, and while civil and human rights groups in the U.S. were pressuring the government to release the Muslims who were being held illegally, another group of people was being transferred to a military prison outside the country.

On Jan. 11, 2002 the first group of alleged al Qaeda and Taliban fighters was arriving on military aircraft at the U.S. naval base at Guantanamo Bay in Cuba. By August of that same year the number of prisoners will rise to 680, representing over 40 countries.

Their transportation from Afghanistan was made with the use of military cargo planes through Turkey. For the duration of the flight—which lasted over 12 hours— the captured alleged fighters were strapped down on the floor of the cargo bay like merchandise, with black hoods and ear muffs on their heads, chains on their legs and their hands tied behind their backs, while a strap was used to pin them down in case of turbulence.

When the planes finally landed at the U.S. naval base in Guantanamo Bay, a new page will be written for human civilization. The time machine was now working at full speed—only backwards.

Photos of the captured alleged al Qaeda and Taliban fighters at the U.S. naval base in Guantanamo Bay—in which they are seen kneeling on the ground with their hand tied behind their backs and wearing orange jumpsuits, masks and ear muffs—were soon published in every news outlet around the globe. The images not only provoked an international fury, but they also openly contested fundamental vested human rights.

The night of January 22, Maria called the journalist and asked for an urgent meeting. Indeed, that same night the journalist went to her house in central Athens. Maria was emphatic, the treatment of the captured alleged al Qaeda and Taliban fighters amounted to torture.

"There were ear muffs, dark goggles, masks, gloves, orange jumpsuits, and restraints on movement," Maria noted. "The ear muffs diminish a person's hearing ability, the gloves his sense of touch, the masks covering the nose and mouth diminish his sense of smell and ability for speech, and the monochrome orange color of their jumpsuits impairs their vision. All together, they amount to sensory deprivation and this is a form of torture."

An article with Maria's interview will be published in Kathimerini English Edition in Greece on January 24 and the next day will be picked up by the International Herald Tribune under the title: "Rights 'Violated' at Guantanamo—Group Says Treatment of Captured al Qaeda and Taliban Fighters May Amount to Torture." Although other rights groups had rushed to criticize the treatment of detainees at the U.S. base in Cuba, it was the first time that a human rights group used specific charges about the treatment of the alleged fighters and that their treatment amounted to torture.

Two days earlier the U.S. Defense Secretary Donald Rumsfeld had brush off international criticism over the detention conditions of Taliban and al Qaeda fighters, declaring that reports by rights groups were "just plain false," and that "no detainee has been mistreated in any way."

The captured alleged fighters are being held in wire cages 2 meters by 2.5 meters (6.5 feet by 8.2 feet) where temperatures during the summer can approach the 38 C (or about 100 F), while they are allowed to exercise only 30 minutes three times per week.

But, the Bush administration remained steadfast on its treatment of the captured alleged Taliban and al Qaeda fighters in Guantanamo Bay, in spite the international condemnation and critical reports filed by specific rights groups that visited the prison camp. Members of the government were stating publicly that if they believed that a prisoner had information about a future terrorist plot then torture could be used in order to disrupt the attack. Indeed, photos of prisoners being carried on stretchers from the interrogation room back to the cells caused fresh criticism.

For Maria this meant a return to an era even before ancient Greece.

"We had solve this problem in the times of ancient Greece with Aristotle, Antiphontas and Dimosthenis, and now we have come to point where we are discussing the same things," observed Maria while noting that it is widely known that a prisoner will always say what his torturers want to hear even if it is not true. "This is what scares me the most, because instead of pushing forward and give solutions to more advanced rights we are returning and contest the basic rights."

As time went by the situation at the U.S. naval base in Guantanamo Bay deteriorated. The prisoners, who lived in open-air cells that had barbed wire for walls—that's why it was named Camp X-Ray—one after another started to go on hanger strike and trying to commit suicide.

Since Jan. 11, 2002, when the first group of detainees arrived at the prison camp, until Jan. 21, 2004 there were 34 suicide attempts. A lawyer who was appointed by the Pentagon to represent an Australian detainee who was captured during fighting in Afghanistan, told reporters on Jan. 21, 2004 that his client's mental state is degenerating after two years of near-solitary confinement. "Mentally, he's probably degenerated to the point where his main concerns are basic human instincts. He desires what he needs: food and shelter," Marine Corps Maj. Michael Mori said according to the Associated Press for his 28-year-old client David Hicks. "Remember, two years, without touch, without outside world communication, it kind of creates a disorientation."

The detention conditions of the captured alleged Taliban and al Qaeda fighters were also condemned by the U.N. Human Rights Committee. "Those detainees, brought shackled, shaved and blindfolded to Cuba, are kept in chain link pens under the constant glare, night and day, of halogen lamps," the committee said in a statement. "The blindfolding, deliberate disorientation, discomfort and constant light are staples of police states all over the world. The idea is to break down the inmate, weaken him from lack of sleep and thereby make him more pliable when the interrogators begin their serious work."

But the prison camp at Guantanamo Bay—where the Bush administration plans to construct some 1,100 cells—was hiding more appalling secrets. On Jan. 29, 2004 the Pentagon announced the release of three detainees from the military prison camp in Cuba. The released alleged fighters were believed to be between the ages of 13 and 15. According to the military, two of the juvenile detainees had been at the Guantanamo prison for as many as two years—meaning that they were arrested when they were 11 years old.

The Pentagon said in a brief statement: "Defense Department senior leadership, in consultation with other senior U.S. government officials, determined that the juvenile detainees no longer pose a threat to our nation, that they have no further intelligence value and that they are not going to be tried by the U.S. government for any crimes."

Although it was known for some time that some of the detainees at the Guantanamo prison where of young age, no one believed that a superpower like the United States would feel threaten by boys as young as 11 and 13 and even imprison them in a military prison camp.

As absurd as this may sound to some, the American government had its own explanation. "Age is not a determining factor in detention," the Pentagon said in the same statement.

One can only wonder what kind of information an 11-year-old boy can have that can be of any value to the U.S. intelligence agencies, or how threatening can this little boy can be to a superpower that has the most technologically-advanced military in the world and has enough nuclear weapons to destroy the entire planet.

According to the Pentagon, two of the three boys were captured during U.S. and allied raids on Taliban camps in Afghanistan, while the third was captured trying to obtain weapons for the Taliban. In other words, a war that started out for the capture of Osama bin Laden has been reduced to the arrest of young boys and the killings of thousands of innocent civilians. And Osama bin Laden is still at large.

The three boys—whose release brought the number of detainees who were released from the Guantanamo prison to 87—were to return to their home countries with assistance of aid groups. The task of resettlement would not be easy because their families, if they are still alive, would have considered their boys dead because all the time that they were in prison their names had not been released by the U.S. military.

For those left behind at Camp X-Ray the future remained uncertain as the Bush administration was pushing hard to have them stand on trial before secret military tribunals, the first to be held by the U.S. in over 50 years.

In April 2005 the New York-based rights group Human Rights Watch released a report in which it stated that reports by FBI agents who witnessed detainee abuse "including chained detainees forced to sit in their own excrement." The rights group says that these recent reports come to be added to the statements of former detainees describing the use of painful stress positions, use of military dogs to threaten detainees, threats of torture and death, and prolonged exposure to extremes of heat, cold and noise.

A month later, in May 2005, violent riots will erupt in Afghanistan and at least 16 Afghans will be killed during mass protests that were triggered by a report in Newsweek magazine, which reported that American soldiers at the Guantanamo prison had thrown a Koran in a toilet and flashed it down. Similar protests will be held across the Arab world, with rioters burning the U.S. flag and copies of the U.S. Constitution outside American embassies and consulates. The following week, Newsweek will retract its earlier report.

"Guantanamo has become the gulag of our times, entrenching the notion that people can be detained without any resource to the law," Amnesty International said in a May 2005 report. "Trials by military tribunals are a parody of justice and law."

Amnesty International was not alone in voicing strong criticism for the detention conditions of the Guantanamo prison camp—also known as Gitmo in the military lingo.

"Shut it down. Just shut it down and the plow it under," wrote the respected journalist Thomas Friedman in a commentary in The New York Times on May 27, 2005. "It has become worse than an embarrassment. I am convinced that more Americans are dying and will die if we keep the Gitmo prison open than if we shut it down. So, please, Mr. President, just shut it down."

As Friedman noted in his commentary, according to reports dozens of detainees have died in U.S. prison camps. "Tell me, how is it that over 100 detainees have died in U.S. custody so far? Heart attacks? This is not just deeply immoral, it is strategically dangerous."

At the same time, the decision by the Bush administration to label the alleged Taliban and al Qaeda fighters as "enemy combatants" or "unlawful combatants" and not as prisoners of war—meaning that they are not entitled to a legal representation and that they may be held indefinitely without charge—was condemned by numerous human rights groups, including the U.N. Commission on Human Rights.

"Locked in their specially built cages at the Guantanamo bay detention camp in Cuba, the al Qaeda and Taliban prisoners have been wondering what kind of justice awaits them," wrote the committee, stressing that the U.S. government should have recognize the detainees as prisoners of war and thus be entitled to the protection of the 1949 Geneva Convention. "To be more precise, prisoners of war are not to be treated like those jailed by the U.S. at its Guantanamo Bay naval base in Cuba."

The U.N. was not alone in saying that the detainees at the Guantanamo deserved more rights. On December 2003 the 9th U.S. Circuit Court of Appeals ruled that Guantanamo prisoners should be allowed to see lawyers and have access to courts. But the prisoners would not be notified of the court's decision as on Jan. 28, 2004 the U.S. Supreme Court granted a request Bush administration to stop the lower court from communicating with a detainee at the Guantanamo prison—temporarily extending the isolation of the prisoners there.

The secret military tribunals were also strongly criticized by military lawyers who were representing some of the detainees at the Guantanamo prison, and who in the legal brief filed with the U.S. Supreme Court on Jan. 14, 2004 argued that the government's plans are unconstitutional.

"Unlike earlier wars, the struggle against terrorism is potentially never-ending," the five lawyers said in their brief according to The Associated Press, effectively challenging the government's sole power to act as jailer, judge and possibly executioner. "If there is no civilian review, the government is free to conduct sham trials and condemn to death those who do nothing more than pray to Allah."

But, tales of alleged abuse and forced confessions became public after the government finally released some of the transcripts from the military tribunals to The Associated Press following a lawsuit that the news agency filed under the Freedom of Information Act.

"As he was hitting me, I kept telling him, no I didn't receive training," a detainee told a military tribunal about his interrogators and torturers. "I was crying and finally I told him I did receive the training. My hands were tied behind my back and my knees were on the ground and my head was bleeding. I was in a lot of pain . . . . At that point, with all my suffering, if he had asked me if I was Osama bin Laden, I would have said yes."

Another detainee said: "Back in Afghanistan I was a simple herdsman. Here in Cuba they thing I am someone important."

So, are these the notorious terrorists who were threatening America?

But, in spite the strong protests from rights groups, foreign governments and even ordinary American citizens over the war in Afghanistan and detention conditions in Abu Ghraib, the Bush administration stood firm on the course that it had taken ever since the terror attacks of 9/11, essentially turning its back to international organizations, international treaties, and even historical allies.

The war on terrorism that President Bush announced four days after the horrific terrorist attacks of September 2003 will enter its second phase. On Feb. 5, 2003, the U.S. Secretary of State Colin Powell goes to the United Nations and declares that the Ansar al-Islam group in southeastern Iraq is the link between al Qaeda, shows satellite photos of warehouses in Iraq where according to U.S. intelligence services Sadam Hussein was hiding weapons of mass destruction, and asks from the Security Council to pass a resolution that would call for military intervention against Iraq.

But, Hans Blix, the U.N.'s chief weapons inspector in Iraq for over a decade was absolute: There was not enough evidence to suggest that Sadam Hussein possessed any such weapons of mass destruction.

"In the Middle Ages when people were convinced there were witches they certainly found them," Blix said on Sept. 18, 2003 as a response to the insistence by the Bush Administration that Iraq was in possession of weapons of mass destruction.

At the same time, the Egyptian President Hosni Mubarak tried to caution the Bush administration that an attack against Iraq would flood the rivers of hatred across the Arab world against the West.

"Instead of having one Osama bin Laden we will have 100 bin Ladens," Mubarak said on March 2003.

The Bush administration turned a deaf ear to all the warnings of caution from its allies and friends, and on March 20 U.S. and British forces will launch a military assault against Iraq without prior approval by the U.N. Security Council.

This action will cast a cloud of doubt over the U.N., the Security Council, and the Council of Europe, as it will directly challenge their reason of existence. The war in Iraq already had its first casualty even before the first smart bomb fell on the ground: the international law and international treaties, upon which a society of nations has been built. If the American government does not feel obliged to respect the rules and regulations of international law and U.N. resolutions, then why Russia should not go back to Chechnya with even a larger military force? Why Israel should not send its entire air force and flatten the Palestinian territories? Why North Korea should not invade South Korea? And why India and Pakistan should not go to an all out war? If a superpower like the United States does not give an example of ethics to the rest of the world, then why should it expect others to respect the very international law that itself has no respect for. If the U.S. does not respect institutions like the United Nations, then why should others respect it?

The military assault against Iraq not only led to the death of thousands of innocent civilians, but it also called into question the existing system of values that the U.N. stands for, and the consequences did not take long before they became violently apparent.

On Aug. 19, 2003, five months after the war against Iraq had started, a powerful explosion will flatten the headquarters of the U.N. mission in Baghdad, killing U.N. envoy Sergio Vieira de Mello along with 21 more workers and injuring over a 100 more. The unprecedented attack against the U.N. will send shockwaves across the international body of nations, an institution that until that day believed that its mission of assisting the weak and vulnerable served as a bulletproof vest for its personnel.

"I probably speak for most of us in saying that the past month has been among the longest and blackest in our lifetime," U.N. Secretary-General Kofi Annan said during a memorial ceremony that was held in New York on Sept. 19, 2003.

"The work of our United Nations colleagues in Iraq was driven solely by a desire to help the Iraqi people build a better future," he added. "When we lost them, our Organization also suffered another loss, of a different kind: a loss of innocence for the United Nations. We, who had assumed that our mission to help others served as its own and ultimate form of protection, now find ourselves threatened and exposed. We, who have tried from the beginning to serve those targeted by violence and destruction, have become a target ourselves. That means we will need to adapt the way we work to our new environment. Wee will have to learn to balance our mission on behalf of other people with the need to protect our own."

Within a few days after the attack the United Nations pulled almost all of its remaining personnel from Iraq, leaving behind only a skeleton staff in order to simply maintain a typical presence on the ground. It was now evident that the war in Iraq not only was a severe blow to international law, but it also created a hostile environment for the work of organizations and institutions that play a vital role in the protection of human rights.

This means that organizations that were responsible for bridging the human rights gap in various countries and regions around the world now were at risk since countries who in the past had been their most vocal advocates and supporters, like the United States, now they are questioning their very existence.

But the downward path that human values had taken ever since 9/11 will not end here. On April 30, 2004 the world will be shocked as national and international media will circulate photographs of American soldiers torturing Iraqi detainees in the Abu Ghraib prison of Baghdad.

"The blatant disregard for international human rights and humanitarian law in the "war on terror" continued to make a mockery of President George Bush's claims that the USA was the global champion of human rights," Amnesty International said in its annual report in May 2005. "Images of detainees in US custody tortured in Abu Ghraib prison in Iraq shocked the world."

The photographs showed American soldiers—men and women—posing next to naked Iraqi detainees who were pilled up on the floor, subjecting them to sexual humiliation and even threatening them with the use of military dogs. In one of the photos that became the subject of strong criticism and condemnation, an Iraqi detainee is shown standing with his back on the wall and a black hood over his head, while electrical cables were attached to his fingers. But perhaps the most tragic of all in this horrific story is that Abu Ghraib was the prison where for decades Iraqis had been tortured by the security forces of Sadam Hussein. Now, it was the turn of their "liberators" to torture them in the exact same facility.

"The night shift was a kind of animal house,'" said former defense secretary James R. Schlesinger in an August 2004 report to the Pentagon. Schlesinger had lead a four-member panel which investigated reports of detainee abuses by U.S. forces in the Abu Ghraib prison in Baghdad. In his 92-page report he will confirm the abuse of some 55 detainees in Abu Ghraib. Another 20 will die in that prison facility.

Schlesinger described the abuse of detainees as "acts of brutality and purposeless sadism." "There was chaos at Abu Ghraib," noted Schlesinger in his report which—contrary to what the Bush administration had been claiming—faulted the Pentagon's top civilian and military leadership for tolerating the kind of abuse that was taking place in Abu Ghraib.

As a result, at least seven U.S. military police officers were facing criminal charges, while more than 12 others were still under investigation. At the same time, nine U.S. Navy Seals were under investigation over the alleged abuse of a detainee named Manadel al-Jamadi, a suspect in the bombing of the Red Cross offices in Baghdad who died in Abu Ghraib prison. He was found hanging from his hands in a toilet.

But prisoner abuse by U.S. forces will also be reported in Afghanistan.

On May 22, 2005 the U.N. envoy to Afghanistan called for the punishment of the American soldiers who were responsible for the death of two Afghan detainees at the Bagram air base in 2002.

"The circumstances involving the abuse and inhumane treatment leading to the death of two Afghan prisoners in Bagram in 2002, reported in the New York Times on the basis of a US army investigation, are deeply disturbing," said Jean Arnault, special representative of the UN secretary-general in Afghanistan.

The incident will also cause a strong condemnation by Afghan President Hamid Karzai. "We are very outraged with this," said Hamid Karzai, the first democratically elected president of Afghanistan. "We want justice."

The next day, on May 23, 2005, the Afghan president will meet with U.S. President George W. Bush at the White House, during which Karzai will ask for the 20,000-strong U.S. forces in Afghanistan to come under the operation control of Afghan forces. The answer that he will get will be far from satisfactory.

"Of course our troops will respond to U.S. commanders," said U.S. President George W. Bush after meeting with Afghan President Hamid Karzai at the White House on May 23, 2005.

During the same month the Bush Administration will again come under fire for its disturbing human rights record. This time it will be by a right group called Physicians for Human Rights, or PHR.

"What the now infamous images from Abu Ghraib do not show is that psychological torture has been at the center of treatment and interrogation of detainees," said Leonard Rubenstein, PHR's Executive Director, in a 135-page report that was released in May 2005 and titled "Break Them Down: Systematic Use of Psychological Torture by US Forces."

"The Bush Administration decided to 'take the gloves off' in interrogations and 'break' prisoners," Rubenstein added.

According to the report, some of psychological torture techniques that were used by the American forces included sensory deprivation, sleep deprivation, forced striping, use of dogs for intimidation, sexual humiliation, mock executions, threats of violence and death threats.

According to human rights groups, some of these techniques continue to be used by U.S. forces even today.

But, the war on terrorism will have one more equally important victim: the refugees. Their situation deteriorated dramatically after the events of 9/11.

After the war in Afghanistan, the International Rehabilitation Council for Torture Victims conducted a study in the Afghan refugee population in neighboring Pakistan and found that 60 percent of them had been tortured in the past. A second study a few months later involving refugees in Norway found that 35 percent of those who had participated in the study were torture victims.

These studies, along with several others conducted by the IRCT in various countries, show an increased number of torture victims among the 12 million refugees around the world. For those people asylum is not an option, its is a right to life.

"The IRCT's experience in post-conflict and port-repressive societies has shown repeatedly that peaceful coexistence and reconciliation requires that the psychological and medical needs of affected populations be expertly addressed," said the anti-torture group in April, 30, 2003.

According to the IRCT, asylum-seekers and refugees have been stigmatized more than anyone else after 9/11. "Although most of them fled their countries to escape from persecution and oppression, many times they are seen as possible terrorists simply because of their country of origin," the IRCT noted. It added that many countries have decreased dramatically the number of asylum requests that they are granting, and as a result thousands of men, women and children are still held in detention centers.

But, the situation raise even more concerns as, according to the IRCT, in many countries the officials who review the asylum applications have received no prior training and are unable to diagnose the psychological trauma that has resulted from torture in many of the asylum-seekers. The IRCT notes that in most cases the asylum-seekers will not even appear in the hearing for their application due to fear, since in the majority of the cases their torturers were state agents.

According to the IRCT, the asylum review process should be conducted by doctors who are trained in diagnosing cases of ill-treatment and torture, while it calls on all countries to adopt and implement the "Istanbul Protocol"[57] which provides detailed and practical international procedures of how to record cases of torture.

Unfortunately the Protocol has been adopted and implemented only by a small number of countries. Thus, refugees and asylum-seekers who are torture victims continue to be trapped in a legal limbo and a bureaucracy that after 9/11 has turned into a dark legal labyrinth.

After 9/11, human rights groups warned that this blunt defiance and sidestepping of international organizations and rule of law by the Bush administration can have devastating consequences in the development of human rights, not only in the West, but across the globe.

---

[57]   The Istanbul Protocol was developed over three years with the involvement of more than 40 organizations from 15 countries, including the IRCT, and in cooperation with over 75 experts on legal, medical, and human rights issues. The Protocol was submitted to the UN High Commissioner for Human Rights on Aug. 9, 1999. Subsequently, the Istanbul Principles have received support in resolutions of the U.N. Human Rights Commission and the U.N. General Assembly. In April 2002, the IRCT entered in a Memorandum of Understanding with the World Medical Association, to work together towards the global implementation of the Istanbul Protocol.

Their fears are being validated day after day. Aside from the military interventions against Afghanistan and Iraq, the torture of detainees and prisoners in Guantanamo Bay and Abu Ghraib, and the prolonged massive detentions of suspects in the United States, the events Bush administration would use the events of 9/11 to serve one more severe blow to human rights: the transport of suspected terrorists from the West to countries which have a dark record of using torture on a large scale.

"Western governments are undermining the global ban on torture by transferring suspects to countries known for routinely torturing prisoners," said the New York-based Human Rights Watch in a joint statement with other seven international rights groups on May 12, 2005.

According to the human rights watchdog, the CIA has transferred some 100 to 150 detainees to countries in the Middle East known to practice torture routinely.

The issue came to the attention of the international press after Maher Arar, a Canadian citizen in transit in New York, was detained by U.S. authorities and sent to Syria. There he remained in Syrian custody without charge and was released ten months later, a period of time, which he said, involved continuous interrogation and repeated torture, often with cables and electrical cords.

Arar's case will not be the only one to see the spotlight. According to the Human Rights Watch, in another case a U.S. government-leased airplane transported two Egyptian suspects who were blindfolded, hooded, drugged, and diapered by hooded operatives, from Sweden to Egypt. There the two men will be held incommunicado for five weeks and tortured with the use of electric shocks.

"Sending suspects to a country where they are likely to be tortured is strictly prohibited by international law," noted the Human Rights Watch in a report on the U.S. rendition program on May 11, 2005. In its report the rights watchdog has gathered information on at least 60 Egyptians who were "rendered" back to Egypt between 1994 and 2005. "Egypt's terrible record of torturing prisoners means that no country should forcibly send a suspect there," the rights group stressed.

On April 28, 2005 President George W. Bush will defend this practice during a press conference, without mentioning Egypt by name. "We operate with the law, and we send people to countries where they say they're not going to torture the people," he said.

But the President's words will be refuted by his own government when on February 2005 the U.S. Department of State in its latest human rights report on Egypt will declare that "torture and abuse of detainees by police, security personnel, and prison guards remained common and persistent," while detailing numerous such cases.

"The Bush administration knows full well that Egypt tortures people in custody, and that its promises not to torture a given suspect are not worth the paper they're written on," the Human Rights Watch noted. "This fig leaf doesn't hide U.S. complicity in the terrible abuses that await suspects sent to Egypt."

Egypt will not be the only country to receive suspects of terrorism from another country. Libya, Syria, Yemen and even Uzbekistan are among those countries that have received such suspects from countries like the United States, Canada, Britain, The Netherlands, Germany, Austria, and Sweden.

There in far away places, in dark, damp basements, dozens and even hundreds of people are being subjected to horrific torture. Many of them after a while will be released, as was in the case of Maher Arar from Canada—since it will be proven that they had absolutely no connection to international terrorism whatsoever. But their release will never undo the physical and psychological pain of those torture victims. Their release will not be able to ease their nightmares. Those people who did nothing wrong will go through a living hell that will mark them for the rest of their lives, while the international law and human rights will remain under a dark cloud of uncertainty.

BREAKING THE SILENCE

It was June 23, 2002 and the journalist along with a doctor from the Medical Rehabilitation Center for Torture Victims in Athens were boarding a flight to Washington DC. The purpose of the trip was the participation in an international conference on torture—perhaps the most notable one in recent years. The element that credited such significance to the event was not as much that it was being held at the heart of the American government in less than a year after the terrorist attacks of 9/11, but the fact that it was bringing together over 50 torture survivors from some 40 countries along with U.S. immigration officials and legislators.

Everyone attending the conference knew that its purpose went beyond from trying to prevent any negative developments in the area of human rights that could follow the 9/11 terrorist attacks. In everyone's eyes the conference was to become a podium for torture victims who would break an undying tradition of silence and walk out of the shadows. Indeed, if something characterized torture all this time—even during the last two decades when numerous countries had ratified the U.N. Convention against Torture—is impunity, which to a certain degree had found an informal asylum in the silence of the victims, who out of shame that resulted from their psychological and physical torment, had become shadows.

But the fear that some human rights could be sacrificed in the name of security after 9/11, made these torture victims to come to America and show the world that they were not ordinary shadows, but shadows of heroes who have a name and a face.

"I am here today to give torture a human face," declared Susan Pineda with a tone of pride in her voice as she stood at the podium, only to burst into tears a few minutes later.

Susan, a former student leader and staunch political and human rights activist in the Philippines, was abducted in 1992 when former President Cory Aquino was in power and taken to a safe house where she was interrogated and tortured. She came here to let the world know what is happening in her country.

"They interrogated me around the clock. They tortured my body. They denied me sleep and sight. They made me hear gunshots and the screams of others. They made me take a bath while they watched me and then they sexually abused me," she said while her tears were still wet on her face.

As Susan recounted the gruesome details of her torture, a blanket of silence covered the auditorium of the Catholic University as the audience sat captivated and shocked. Nothing in the appearance of this beautiful young woman alluded to the fact that she was a torture victim. The audience listened very carefully to every word she said and every move she made, admiring her courage of sharing publicly those dark memories, but also feeling apologetic on behalf of the human race that marched through her soul like a ruthless army that pillages and burns entire villages and towns.

After her release, Susan was forced to falsely confess that she was a surrendering rebel. But the nightmare didn't end there. Agents continued to follow her for over three months, calling her at home and making threats on her life, in an effort to force her to withdraw the case she had filed at the Commission of Human Rights. Today she works as a paralegal and a counselor, while she has also served as an elected city councilor of Angeles City in Pampanga, the Philippines. She still hopes that one day she will see her torturers pay for their crimes so she could have closure.

Then maybe the nightmares will stop.

Susan was the first survivor to take the microphone at the two-day conference, tiled "Help End Torture—On the Question of Torture: An Exchange of Views," and organized by the US-based Torture Abolition and Survivors Support Coalition (TASSC) International—the only organization founded entirely by torture survivors.

Next at the podium was a couple, Patricio Rice and Fatima Cabrera. Patricio was born in Ireland and soon after he joined the Divine Missionaries, he moved to Argentina. There he later joined the Little Brothers of the Gospel of Charles de Foucauld, and in 1975 he begun working in a shantytown in Buenos Aires. When the military seized power in the country the following year, he became active in denouncing the repression, particularly against church people. In 1976, he was picked up by soldiers, together with a young church worker, Fatima.

"They forced us inside a car and took us to a detention center at a 'no-peasants land,'" he told a silent audience. "We were tortured to be destroyed." United in their humiliation and hatred, they both had been blindfolded and kept in the dark while they were being tortured.

"Torture has no limits to what they can do to you," said Fatima, who was seated next to Patricio. "They applied electric shocks to the most sensitive parts of our bodies, including the eyes and the genitalia."

She declared that their interrogators "were only interested in extracting information from us; they were not paying any attention to our pleas." Fatima noted that because she was suffering from asthma there would be doctors in the room during her torture, who would intervene and assist her during an asthma attack so that the torture could continue. Their 'interrogators' continued to torture them by placing them naked on the cement floor in uncomfortable positions, with hoods on their heads and leather straps securing their feet.

"Every time they would pull us up we would start to suffocate," she noted while describing only a few of their torture sessions. Fatima explained that the torture was ongoing, continuing even when they were showering. "These are humans who carry out the torture against other humans, so it is the responsibility of the entire human race to put an end to torture," she said.

Patricio was released a couple of months after the intervention of the Irish ambassador, who had been informed of his incarceration by eyewitnesses at the site where the soldiers picked them up. Fatima, who was still in her teens when she was imprisoned by the military, remained in prison until 1979. In 1985 the two were reunited, and after a few months he resigned from the priesthood and they got married.

"We must overcome our fear and tell the truth to our families about what we really went through. We must feel again that we are in control," declared Marvyn Perez from Guatemala, who was arrested and tortured when he was 14 years old.

Born in a farming community, Marvyn in 1981 joined a student movement that was fighting for a better educational system and for end to human rights violations. The following year he was illegally arrested by police officers who snatched him from inside a bus. He was taken to a police station where for the next three days he would be subjected to round-the-clock interrogation. Then his 'interrogators' blindfolded him and took him to an undisclosed building where he was brutally tortured.

"I believed that I was living the last days of my life," Marvyn said before a silent audience. His torturers kicked him, punched him, administered electroshocks, and caused burns in various parts of his body. Twelve days later he was released after they forced him to sign a statement in which he acknowledged that he was a member of a resistance group. As a result of that coerced confession, his family would no longer talk to him.

"The attitude of the people around me had changed," Marvyn noted. He was not the only one who found himself socially isolated after being torture and stigmatized.

"I had three first cousins who committed suicide following their torture," said Fahima Vorgetts from Afghanistan, explaining that in her culture for a man the price of shame has greater social dimensions than personal.

"I have members of my family who are in prison because they were tortured," she added, noting that men would rarely talk about their torture. Fahima, who now lives in the U.S., stressed that prior to 9/11 nobody paid attention to the human rights violations that were taking place in Afghanistan.

"The September 11th was a tragedy for America, but for Afghanistan every day of the last 23 years has been a tragedy," Fahima declared.

One of the issues that was raised at the conference was the stance of the United States on human rights issues in the wake of the terrorist attacks of September 11 last year. Concerns over the conduct of the Bush administration were voiced not only by survivors, but also by American lawmakers, such as Congressman Jim Moran, a Democrat from the state of Virginia.

Moran criticized the Bush administration's decision to withdraw the country's signature from the UN criminal court, saying that it was "wholly perverse." He added:

"It was very disappointing, as was the declared withdrawal. It is embarrassing." The congressman said that the United States has a "very stained record when it comes to using the leverage that it has in order to promote and further human rights," stressing that instead it spends billions of dollars on the military. "We now have more military capability than all the other countries combined," he noted.

Congressman Moran stressed that the time for talk has ended, and that action needs to be taken by lawmakers and the administration in a bipartisan way. He said that more money is needed to create rehabilitation centers for torture victims in the United States, a country that has over 500,000 torture survivors on its soil.

"You have to walk the walk and not just talk the talk, and so far all we have done is talk," he said, stressing that if nothing is done "it will come back to haunt us."

On the sidelines of the three-day conference the journalist had the opportunity to meet with Katrin, an Iraqi woman who had recently moved to the U.S. Katrin was a survivor of a chemical attack by the forces of Saddam Hussein back in 1987, and for years was a guest at Maria's house in Greece.

"It was the summer of April 17, 1995, and I was in my office at the Medical Rehabilitation Center for Torture Victims waiting to examine several asylum-seekers who had recently arrived to Greece," Maria told the journalist about the day she met Katrin. "Among the many people who were waiting in the next room was a woman who was wearing a blue jean, a white T-shirt, and big smile across her face, making me wonder if she was truly a victim. She was the picture of life and joy."

But this bright smile was only a cover for the incredible pain—both physical and mental—that was hidden inside Katrin, and Maria was about to come face-to-face with it.

"She told me that she was in northern Iraq with a group of Kurds, the only survivors of a chemical attack by the forces of Saddam Hussein. I was shocked because I knew that thousands of Kurds—men, women, and children—were killed in that attack," Maria said. "Knowing the long-term effects of chemicals I started to worry about the fate of this woman, evaluating that the trembling of her hands, the pain in the knees and the joints, as well as the difficulty of breathing, were the first signs of a syndrome that had was definitely manmade."

With no place to live in Athens, Maria offered to have her stay at her house and to work as a translator at the torture rehab center. "So, Katrin became the fifth member of my family for about three years and then she left for America," said Maria who could not come to the conference because of the sudden death of her father.

Katrin, a former geology professor at the University of Baghdad, now works for a government agency that deals with human rights issues and lives alone in a small apartment in Washington D.C. Living away from relatives, the closest ones live in Michigan and Canada, Katrin was very pleased to see the two visitors from Greece—although she was clearly disappointed that Maria did not make it. She had even bought gifts for all the members of Maria's family as a gesture of gratitude that she was filling even after all those years for the people who helped her stand on her own feet again.

Katrin, a relatively tall woman with brunette hair and large glasses that cover most of her face, belongs to the group of survivors who believe that victims should break their silence and tell their traumatic stories publicly.

"This is the introduction to the book that I will be publishing in a few months," Katrin said as she handed a small pack of computer-printed pages to the journalist and while preparing to serve a traditional Iraqi meal for her guests.

Although the journalist had prior knowledge about Katrin prior to their meeting, after reading the introduction that she had written for her book he felt a lump coming up his throat. In front of him was a woman who had spent seven years with Kurdish rebels in the mountains of northern Iraq, survived a horrific chemical attack by the forces of Saddam Hussein, and escaped two attempts on her life in Algeria because she was a Christian.

Katrin started to write the book when she was still living in the study room of Maria's house. "After three tranquil and therapeutic years, Katrin came and told me that she could no longer take advantage of my hospitality and that she had to get a job," Maria said about how the idea for the book came about. "I did not respond immediately, but after a while I returned and gave her a pack of white pages and a pen and asked her to sit down and write and story of her life. I told her that this would be the greatest offering that she could make to her people. Within a month she had written more than 500 pages in Arabic."

As a gesture of gratitude, Katrin asked Maria to write the forward, and Maria accepted. Somewhere in the forward Maria writes: "For life and death the world is one. And for Katrin, who as a citizen of this world was born in Baghdad and not in America, death has been chasing her for a long time but so far she has managed to elude him. She is a survivor."

But, this brief trip to Washington D.C. will include one more surprise for the journalist. On the afternoon of the first day of the conference he was to attend an award ceremony for Athony Reeler—founder and executive director of the non-governmental group Amani Trust in Harare, Zimbabwe—who had recently escape from the country following a raid to his office by government forces.

The journalist had heard a lot about Reeler and his human rights organization but had not met him until that day. The Amani Trust has treated torture survivors and documented cases of torture and ill-treatment in Zimbabwe since 1993, in spite the constant threats from the Mugabe's regime.

Reeler was to receive the 2002 Eclipse Award from the U.S.-based Center for Torture Victims for his extraordinary service on behalf of torture survivors. The ceremony was held at one of the buildings of U.S. Congress. Arriving a little late, the journalist saw Reeler standing next to a congressman from California who was already at the podium.

Slim-built and dressed in a suit that seemed to be his first after a long time, Reeler looked humble and had a distant look as if his mind was back in Harare and the victims that now were without the help of his organization. To the journalist it was obvious that Reeler had grown accustomed to live side-by-side the victims that he was treating and far away from places where one would need to wear a tie in order to enter. But he felt that he had to attend the ceremony, not so much for his personal recognition but for that of his human rights organization and his colleagues in Harare who daily risked their lives in order to offer their humanity and care to those who needed it the most.

"Mr. Reeler has offered a great service to the people of Zimbabwe by uncovering the evil that has taken root in Zimbabwe," said U.S. Congressman Edward Royce from California who was also chairman of the House Subcommittee on Africa. "From January until today, more than 450 citizens of Zimbabwe have been tortured and many more have been killed or 'disappeared.' Anthony Reeler and his associates have unmasked the government of Robert Mugabe. Their effort is recognized around the world, as it should."

With the help of people like Reeler and the courage of torture victims like Pineda and others, the silence that covered torture has finally broken, striping away the mask of hypocrisy from oppressing regimes that continue to use torture as a method of terrorizing the citizens of their countries.

The silence has broken!

IN THE SHADOWS
OF ASYLUM

The war against terrorism has proven disastrous for human rights worldwide, not only because it has resulted in the death of thousands of innocent people and weakened human rights, but also because it led to major changes in the immigration policies of most Western nations—including Greece. As a result, tens of thousands of refugees and asylum-seekers are trapped in the shadows of a legal system that is under ongoing transformation, adjusting according to the situation and creating a new kind of cultural racism.

The first signs appeared in 2002, when in Greece—a country that traditionally has been a hub for refugees and asylum-seekers due to its geographic location—there was a dramatic decrease in the number of people who were granted refugee status or asylum[58].

The office of U.N. High Commissioner for Refugees (UNHCR) in Athens in its 2002 report about Greece noted that during the year the country gave asylum to just 1% of the Iraqis who had filed an application, compared to an average of 47% among EU countries.

The percentages were so low[59] that the Greek government had to go as far as to give informal assurances to the UNHCR representative in the country that no Iraqis—including rejected asylum seekers—will be deported, in accordance with a UNHCR global moratorium on forced returns to Iraq.

---

[58] According to the records of the Greek Ministry of Public Order, the first five months of 2002 there were some 1,857 applications for asylum—of which 772, or 41%, were from Iraqi refugees—and until June the government had approved only 18 cases. The previous year, 2001, the Greek government had granted asylum to some 295 refugees and had rejected as many as 1,165 applications—a fact that brings Greece at the bottom of the European Union in terms of the protection it offered to refugees seeking asylum.

[59] According to the UN High Commissioner for Refugees, in 2002 the Greek state rejected as many as 9,278 applications for asylum, a year that Iraqis accounted for 45% of all claims.

"This means that genuine refugees may be left without international protection and be at risk of forcible return to their country of origin with possible tragic consequences for their lives," the UNHCR office in Greece said in a statement.

That meant that people like Ayiad from Iraq who had survive the most horrendous torture under the regime of Saddam Hussein and who had sold all their belongings to travel like a pack of animals as cargo on a boat or a truck in order to come to Greece, were learning the toughest way that in the 'developed world' compassion has diplomatic and political dimensions.

The refugee all of a sudden had become the object of international political, legal, and diplomatic debate and negotiations. Countries in Europe and elsewhere were engaged in fierce renegotiation of asylum—an issue that had been legally defined by the United Nations years ago. The doors of European countries were slowly closing one after another, sending a thundering message worldwide. Europe would soon become known to rest of the world by its nickname: "The fortress."

The first symptoms of this new immigration policy appeared in early 2003, a year that was marked by a sheer decline[60] in the arrival of asylum-seekers in developed countries.

"This was the lowest total since 1997, and the third lowest total since 1988," wrote Robert White in an analysis for this book. At the time White was the UNHCR representative in Greece. "In the European Union, the number of asylum-seekers dropped 22 per cent from the previous year, to 288,000. This was also the lowest since 1997."

It was clear that the message sent by the developed countries had reached its receiver, and it was saying: "Don't come here. You are not welcome."

If this had happen a few years earlier, then Lomeny, a 26-year-old woman from the war-ravaged Sudan who now lives as a refugee in Greece, perhaps wouldn't be alive today—an unfortunate fate that under the current conditions will be met by many future refugees.

The journalist met Lomeny on March 14, 2001, a few months before the terrorist attacks in the U.S. The interview had been arranged by the UNHCR in cooperation with the Greek Council for Refugees, in light of the World Refugee Day. The journalist wanted to write an article about the vital importance of asylum for a refugee, in hope that the story would come to be added in the general discussion of immigration that had already started in the gulfs of the European Union.

A Christian in a country dominated by the Islamic faith and Sunni Muslims, Lomeny was considered a member of an underclass with meager rights, both because of her religion and gender.

---

[60]   According to the records of the U.N. High Commissioner of Refugees, in 2003 the number of asylum-seekers in 36 developed countries declined by 20%, reaching a total of 463,000.

She was caught in the middle of a two-decades-old civil war pitting black Christians and animists in the south against the Arab Muslims of the north, which has cost more than 2 million lives and led to the displacement of over 4 million people. Amid daily clashes in the south, Lomeny and her family fled to the capital Khartoum in the early '90s, joining a drove of internally displaced people. There, Lomeny managed to get a job as a secretary at the local Christian church in 1995. Her new job gave her a second chance to rebuild her life. The church was attended regularly by a number of families from the local Christian community, and soon they opened a kindergarten adjacent to the church. After three years in the job, her life took another positive turn—she got married.

But all this changed one day in 1998 when a foreign journalist came up to her and asked her for an interview.

"I was working at a Christian church as a secretary, and one day a foreign journalist came there to ask me about our situation because we are at war. He asked me about our situation and I told him," Lomeny noted during her interview with the journalist in Athens.

Little did she know that speaking to a foreign journalist would cause havoc in her life.

"The next day security forces came and arrested me and took me to the prison," she said in a strained voice, while maintaining eye contact. "They said that I was giving secrets and information to the foreign journalist."

Lomeny, whose real name has been concealed to protect her identity, spent two days in prison. She offers few details on the conditions of her incarceration. When asked if she had been mistreated by members of the security forces, she lowered her eyes and voice and replied, "No."

Not long after her release from prison, government security forces mounted a campaign of intimidation against the Christian community and destroyed the church. "After two or three months they destroyed the church, because they said the Muslims in the area did not want the church," Lomeny said. "After they destroyed the church there was a protest and (the security forces) said that I was the leader and came and arrested me again."

The second time she was arrested only for one day. Again she denied any mistreatment on the part of the security forces, and said nothing of the conditions of her detention. But she did say that after her second arrest she was shaken. "I was afraid for my life, because some people when they are arrested like that, they disappear," she said and the fear that she had felt then was again reflected on her face.

Her fear was not groundless. For decades, human rights advocacy groups have been filing reports naming government security forces as responsible for a number of extrajudicial killings and disappearances of opposition followers and members of religious minorities. Women above all have been the subject of discrimination and abuse. Sudan has yet to ratify the 1981 U.N. Convention on the Elimination of All Forms of Discrimination Against Women. President Omar Hassan Ahmad al-Bashir in January 2001 refused once again to ratify the treaty because "it contradicts family principles and behavior" and Sudan could do without "such strange practices."

It was after her second arrest that she decided that she was no longer safe in Sudan and that she had to flee the country—illegally.

"My husband's colleagues helped me, suing illegal methods," Lomeny explained to the journalist. She and her husband were hidden inside a truck and were taken across the northern border to Egypt. There, they spend six months before arrangements were made for them to cross illegally into Greece. The passage would not come cheap. "For me it was a lot of money, because I paid $1,000," she said.

Lomeny landed in Greece on June 6, 1999 along with her husband, and after evading the detection by authorities they managed to register with the Greek Council for Refugees (GCR). Two years later they were still striving to make a living, on minimum financial support by GCR, as she was still unemployed and her husband had a part-time job.

But she is not ungrateful.

"I didn't come looking for a better life," Lomeny noted. "At least I am safe here." Those last few words of Lomeny comprise the entire meaning that asylum has for the refugees, people who fled their countries because they didn't want to give up their right to life.

Asylum in Europe

In Europe, the issue of asylum especially after 9/11 was brought at the top of the political agenda. The large movements of economic migrants and trafficking victims convinced some politicians, journalists, and citizens that their countries were literally under siege and constant threat.

Raymond Hall, head of UNHCR's Europe bureau, described 2003 as a "worrying year" with countries introducing increasingly restrictive measures and shrill rhetoric sometimes drowning out rational debate.

In Britain, the shadow home secretary, Oliver Letwin, promised that if his Conservative party were to win the upcoming elections he would make sure that all asylum seekers arriving in Britain will be immediately deported to a "far offshore processing" island. Letwin made those comments during a party conference in Blackpool on Oct. 7, 2003, during which he stressed that all asylum seekers who reach Britain will find the door closed. "We will replace the present asylum system—in its entirety—with a system of quotas for genuine refugees and the offshore processing of all claims, to deter all but genuine claims for protection from persecution," the British daily *The Guardian* quoted him as saying.

In Switzerland, the right-wing Swiss People's Party (SVP) won 26.6% of the vote in the 2003 national elections, mainly because of its anti-foreigner campaign in which asylum seekers were portrayed as criminals and drug dealers. One of its campaign posters was featuring caricatured features of a black man and the slogan: "SWISS ARE THE NEGROES OF SWITZERLAND," the *Time Magazine* reported on Oct. 12, 2003.

In this climate, the number of asylum seekers in Europe in 2003 declined sharply, although according to the UNHCR the decrease may have been facilitated by an improving situation in places like Afghanistan, Iraq, Serbia and Montenegro.

In spite all that, tens of thousands of people knocked on the door of the Old Continent. Many of them founded airtight closed, while others died before even reaches its shores.

On Oct. 25, 2003 a fishing trawler that was carrying some 50 fatigued African immigrants sank before reaching the Spanish shores. The first bodies will be found a week later. "Rescue teams have recovered the bodies of 20 people off southern Spain following a shipwreck involving would-be immigrants last weekend," the Associated Press reported on Oct. 31, 2003. According to officials, all bodies retrieved were North African men. Three more bodies were washed up a week later, making everyone to ask one question: "How many died?" The answer to that question will come a few days later when the waves will bring to shores several more bodies, bringing the final death toll to 32 people. According to the Moroccan immigrant worker's association (ATIME), some 4,000 would-be immigrants had drowned in the past five years in their effort to cross into Europe by crossing the treacherous Strait of Gibraltar, the Associated Press reported on Nov. 3, 2003.

In the Old Continent, the countries[61] that received the bulk of asylum seekers in 2003 were the United Kingdom, France and Germany, according to UNHCR statistics. But, although these countries did receive the most asylum applications across Europe, they marked a substantial decrease[62] that reached the 41%.

On Feb. 21, 2004, the UN High Commissioner for Refugees, Ruud Lubbers, in a statement noted that particularly in Europe, the heated debate on asylum and the hardening of attitudes were to a considerable extent driven by the high numbers that arrived during the 1990s. "Now that the numbers have dropped back to the levels we were seeing in the late 1980s, I hope the debate will focus once again on the vital need to protect refugees, as well as the need to find permanent solutions for them, and better ways to share the burden among states," he said.

But this optimism of the High Commissioner will not last long. A month later he will be forced to raise the tone again after watching the European Union working

---

[61]   According to the UNHCR, in 2003 the United Kingdom received some 61,050 asylum applications, followed by France with 51,400 asylum requests, and Germany with 50,450.

[62]   In 2003 there was a decline in the number of asylum applications that traditionally were asylum receivers. In the United Kingdom there was a decrease by 41%, while in Germany the year was marked by a 29% drop—its lowest total in 19 years.

on two draft directives that would reduce even further the number of refugees and asylum seekers on its soil.

"Europe should be proud of its tradition of giving asylum, of saving lives," Lubbers said on March 29, 2003, a week after he had sent a letter to the Irish Prime Minister, Bertie Ahern, whose country had the six-month rotating presidency of the European Union at the time. "The numbers of asylum seekers are going down. We're working hard to find solutions and improve conditions in regions of origin, and we are seeing the successes of that humane policy and its effect on the numbers moving onwards. It would be a real pity if Europe, at this point, were to undermine the great tradition of protecting real refugees."

Lubbers also raised a number of major concerns about the proposed draft of the Qualification Directive, including the proposals to severely limit the scope of what constitutes "serious harm," and therefore who qualifies as a beneficiary of international protection. He stressed that these could lead to people fleeing a war zone being rejected from all forms of international protection.

The UNHCR also expressed a range of concerns, including the proposed application of the so-called "safe third country" concept under which asylum seekers may be sent back to another country designated as "safe." The refugee agency criticized it as a "sweeping exemption" that would deny certain asylum seekers access to a procedure altogether, disregarding the possibility that a country generally considered safe "might nonetheless not be safe for particular individuals." This would thereby create a real danger of indirect forced return of refugees to possible persecution in their home country "in contravention of the 1951 Convention and other international human rights law instruments."

Lubbers described the criteria for determining the "safety" of a third country as "minimalist" and warned that such procedures could lead to asylum seekers being sent back to countries that do not maintain basic human rights standards, and where there is no guarantee their cases would be fairly and efficiently examined.

"The cumulative effect of these proposed measures is that the EU will greatly increase the chances of real refugees being forced back to their home countries," Lubbers noted. "It will be hard to track, because the forced return may take place via a chain of countries, but that does not mean it will not happen. Even a single person being sent back to the risk of torture is one too many."

Lubbers stressed that if the EU adopted the Directives in their current form it would set a negative precedent for other parts of the world, where they would be perceived as an effort to shift the burden back to developing countries which already host the great majority of the world's refugees. "This could have a knock-on effect that might weaken the protection of refugees all across the world," he said. "Other countries will look at the EU and say 'If they can do this, so can we.'

Lubbers concluded: "We need to remember the original intentions of the harmonization process, which was to produce a common European asylum system, based—and here I quote the Tampere Conclusions—'on the absolute respect for the right to seek asylum' and the 'full and inclusive application' of the 1951 UN Refugee Convention. We need to revive that spirit."

On Nov. 5, 2004, the European heads of state adopted the "Hague Program," which takes up the challenge for taking forward the Common European Asylum System. The "program" provides for the establishment of the common asylum procedure and uniform status for those granted asylum or subsidiary protection, based on a thorough and complete evaluation of the legal instruments adopted in the first phase. Under the plan, the European Commission is invited to adopt second phase instruments of the Common European Asylum System with a view to adoption by 2010.

Asylum in Greece

In contrast with the rest of Europe, Greece saw a marked increase[63] in the number of asylum applications during 2003.

"But what does this mean exactly for Greece?" asked Robert White, the UNHCR representative in Greece in an essay that he wrote for this book. "This is a critical time for refugees and asylum-seekers in Greece and in Europe. Migration and asylum issues are of fundamental interest and importance to Greece and its people because the socio-demographic landscape of the country changed radically in the past ten years. One reason for this is the traditional hospitality of the Greek people, receiving those who come for diverse reasons ranging from economic betterment to safety from persecution. A second reason is the linkage for many Greeks to their own personal or family refugee history. And a third, important reason concerns Greece's location at the external border of the European Union."

White explains that about "one million or more non-Greeks live and work alongside ten million Greeks today. Of the one million, an estimated 17,000 persons are refugees and asylum-seekers."

But how are these figures arrived at?

According to White, over the past twenty years about 7,000 persons received either refugee status or humanitarian status in Greece, and the UNHCR estimates that about 4,000 remain in Greece. Additionally, there are an estimated 5,000 persons, registered prior to 2003, who are still in the asylum system—awaiting decisions on their asylum claims.

"Added to this figure would be thousands of persons who have expressed their wish to seek protection in Greece and are awaiting official registration," he notes.

---

[63] According to the office of the UN High Commissioner for Refugees in Athens, some 8,178 asylum applications were filed in Greece—a 45% increase from the 2002 figure of 5,664 asylum applications, and the most since 1990. The UNHCR notes that part of the increase is also due to accelerated registrations by the authorities of persons who had arrived in Greece in 2002.

"These various categories of persons are all of concern to UNHCR, although relatively few are granted refugee or humanitarian status."

Analyzing the recent refugee trends, White emphasizes that since 1990 the predominant countries of origin for asylum-seekers have been Iraq, Turkey, and Iran. More recently Afghanistan has supplanted Iran and Turkey, after Iraq. He stresses that nearly half of all asylum-seekers registered in 2002 were from Iraq.

In terms of Greece's asylum regime and overall immigration policy, the government at the time was waiting for a new legal framework from the EU that was still being debated in Brussels.

"With that goal in mind, UNHCR entered into dialogue over the past few months with main Greek partner agencies, who were supportive of issues and concerns relating to refugees and asylum-seekers," White said. "The result is a document[64] entitled "UNHCR Position on Important Aspects of Refugee Protection in Greece"."

Some of the basic concerns of the UN refugee agency in Greece in terms of the country's asylum process included: access to the Greek asylum procedure; detention and reception center capacities and conditions; improving provision for legal aid; the low refugee recognition rates; the need for an independent appeals process for asylum-seekers; and special issues relating to refugee women and refugee children.

"UNHCR Greece has recently observed with great concern the decrease in the number of refugees granted refugee status, in accordance with the 1951 Geneva Convention, or with humanitarian status, an alternative form of protection," White said. "Although in 2001 the recognition rate for those granted refugee and humanitarian status was 22.4 per cent, the 2002 overall recognition rate dropped dramatically to 1.0 per cent, or 100 persons. The same trend appears in 2003, when there was an overall recognition rate 0.6%, or 28 persons."

These numbers are disheartening.

"These refugee recognition rates are among the lowest in the EU, which registered an average of 18.4% overall in 2002," White noted.

But the complaints of the UN refugee agency do not end there. "In 2003, UNHCR observed with concern the reduced capacity and financial resources to accommodate asylum-seekers in reception centers, with the closure of three of the twelve such facilities," White adds. "With over 8,000 asylum applications lodged in 2003, the overall capacity of reception centers is now less than 1,200 places—inadequate to meet basic needs of the majority."

---

[64]   The document produced by the office of the UN High Commissioner for Refugees in Greece covered five central themes: a) improving the national asylum system, b) contributing to the harmonization of asylum law and policy within the EU, c) advancing Greek asylum and migration law, d) facilitating durable solutions for refugees and other persons of concern to UNHCR, e) supporting refugee work in Greece and UNHCR's work with refugees in other parts of the world.

On May 1, 2004 the journalist went to the eastern Aegean island of Samos for an immigration story ahead of Greece's Olympic Games. The island marks the closest sea border with Turkey and is one of the favorite smuggling routes for human traffickers.

As part of the story the journalist went on two coast guard patrol tours, one during the day and one at night. "This is the closest (island) point to Turkey," noted Ensign Ioannis Mozas as he pointed to the Turkish islet known as Aghios Nikolaos to Greeks and Baytak Adasi to Turks. "It is just 1.2 kilometers (0.7 miles)."

Samos is so close to the Turkish shore that some immigrants have swum across wearing flippers or floated aboard children's plastic boats or makeshift wooden rafts. Other times, smugglers have ferried them on fishing boats, sailboats and even speedboats that can make the trip in a matter of minutes.

"Some 200 illegal immigrants are being detained daily . . . on the island of Samos," Angelos Tsigris, a professor of criminology at the police academy, said during a 2004 conference.

In 2003, Greek coast guard detained over 2,400 illegal immigrants and arrested more than 70 smugglers across Greece. Although the figure is significantly smaller compared to 2001, when some 6,800 immigrants were detained, experts believe that for every immigrant detained another manages to get through.

On the island there is a "Reception Center" for illegal immigrants, one of several that are criticized in the reports of UNHCR office in Greece. Of course the title—and especially the word "reception"—sound very nice and one can picture images of well-treated illegal immigrants who enjoy the hospitality of the Greek state. In reality, though, the so-called "Reception Center" is a detention facility operated by a special branch of the police.

Of course the journalist when he visited the center with a photographer was clearly unaware of the fact that facility was a prison. After ringing the bell the journalist was about to confirm what White had been complaining about in his reports.

The large metallic gray door opened and a surprised police officer came face-to-face with the journalist and the photographer. But in shock was also the journalist who was taken aback by a sickening stench that was coming from inside and by observing scores of scruffy detainees who had gathered in the yard to see the visitors, and who were clearly living in primitive and filthy conditions.

The police officer quickly explained that in order to enter the facility the journalist would have to have a written authorization from the police headquarters and then he shut the door. But this was enough time for the journalist to get an idea of the living conditions inside the facility, which in the past housed a police station.

A confirmation of his understanding of the situation will come a while later when the police commander in charge of the prison—also known as "Reception Center"—will refuse him access to the facility because as he said: "How do I know that you don't have a hidden camera somewhere?"

Of course this was never an issue because the journalist was working for an reputed international news agency that does not use such practices and the photographer that was accompanying him was holding his camera in his hands. But the reaction of the police commander was the best confirmation that the authorities had something to hide.

But what made the conditions in the "Reception Center" on Samos even more alarming is that among the dozens of detainees there could be victims of torture who had fled their countries to avoid persecution.

"It is likely that torture victims may encounter degrees of hardship similar to other asylum-seekers—whether in detention or reception centers or in legal status, including refugee recognition rates," White declared.

With the conditions in places like Iraq and Afghanistan still being challenging, the UN refugee agency notes that the time for complete repatriation has not come yet.

"UNHCR seeks cooperation with the Greek Government in support of the eventual return of refugees and asylum-seekers, once conditions prove more viable—although it is recognized that security conditions in these countries does not permit repatriation at the present time," White said.

The Day After

For human rights the future is rather gloomy and uncertain, with the war against terror continuing and millions of refugees and asylum seekers filling unwanted as they find airtight doors in front them in almost every developed country they visit.

Today, over 1 billion people don't have access to clean water; over 121 children don't have access to basic education; and over 500,000 women die every year due to pregnancy complications. In 2004, some 25 million people remained internally displaced in their countries, and the UN refugee agency had to capacity to assist just 6 million of them. At the same time, the fate of some 534,000 uprooted people who had found refuge in Serbia and Montenegro remains uncertain, as the ethnic and religious hatred in parts of the Balkans is lurking like a sniper who is waiting for the right moment to pull the trigger. In central Asia, the 112,000 refugees who fled from tiny kingdom of Bhutan a decade ago remain in refugee camps in neighboring Nepal. The two-decade-old civil war in Colombia, which by 2004 had caused the uprooting of more than 3 million people, remains the worst humanitarian disaster in the Western hemisphere. Hundreds of thousands of refugees from Burundi and Somalia in East Africa remain trapped in a legal vacuum that is perpetuated by an economic and political instability in the area. At the same time, hundreds of prisoners at the U.S. naval base in Guantanamo Bay, Cuba, have been subjected to ill-treatment and torture, and remain in isolation from the rest of the world.

In the annual report for 2004, Amnesty International Secretary-General, Irene Khan, wrote in the foreword: "In 1973 AI published its first report on torture. It found that: 'torture thrives on secrecy and impunity. Torture rears its head when the legal barriers against it are barred. Torture feeds on discrimination and fear. Torture gains ground when official condemnation of it is less than absolute.' The pictures of detainees in US custody in Abu Ghraib, Iraq, show that what was true 30 years ago remains true today."

But, the future could have been even more gloomy—perhaps even dark like a moonless night in the desert—if it wasn't for people like Maria, Anthony Reeler and Katrina on one hand, people who have experienced the suffering and who are defenders of human rights, and on the other hand the increasing number of torture victims who find the strength and courage to tell their stories publicly and expose those oppressing regimes worldwide.

"Listen to the voices of the victims, and respond to their cry for justice," Irene Khan noted.

It is their stroke of the brush and those of human rights groups that are applied on the global canvas of human rights and make it less dark. It is them who stand guard as the last line of defense for human values that are under a constant attack. Of course, we should never forget those who lost their lives in far away places while offering humanitarian assistance to fellow humans. We should always be grateful for their sacrifice and selfless generosity. Humanity is poorer without them!

www.ingramcontent.com/pod-product-compliance
Lightning Source LLC
Chambersburg PA
CBHW030409290526
45785CB00004B/1948